4TH AND GOAL

4TH AND GOAL

Coaching for life's tough calls

BILL McCARTNEY

Tyndale House Publishers, Inc.
WHEATON, ILLINOIS

Visit Tyndale's exciting Web site at www.tyndale.com

4th and Goal

Copyright © 2002 by Promise Keepers. All rights reserved.

Cover photograph © 2002 by Myron/Getty Images. All rights reserved.

Cover photograph of men © 2002 by Lois Gervais/Corbis Images. All rights reserved.

Author photo by Wayne Armstrong, copyright © 2002 by Promise Keepers. All rights reserved.

Designed by Ron Kaufmann

Edited by Dave Lindstedt

Scripture quotations are taken from the *Holy Bible,* New International Version®. NIV®. Copyright © 1973, 1978, 1984 by International Bible Society. Used by permission of Zondervan Publishing House. All rights reserved.

Library of Congress Cataloging-in-Publication Data

McCartney, Bill date.
  4th and goal : coaching for life's tough calls / Bill McCartney.
    p. cm.
Includes bibliographical references.
ISBN 0-8423-7044-7 (alk. paper)
1. Christian men—Religious life. 2. Fathers—Religious life. I. Title: Fourth and goal.
II. Title.
BV4529.17 .M33 2002
248.8'42—dc21   2002002096

Printed in the United States of America

08 07 06 05 04 03 02
7   6   5   4   3   2   1

Contents

SINGLES & RELATIONSHIPS

CHARACTER

THE INTERNET & PORNOGRAPHY

SANCTITY OF LIFE

BUSINESS ETHICS

FINANCIAL INTEGRITY

SPORTS ETHICS

Fatherhood

ADVICE FOR PARENTS OF TEENS

How are we to deal with our teenagers? Here's what Mark Twain suggested: "When a child turns thirteen, you put him in a barrel with only a hole to feed him through. When he turns eighteen, plug the hole." It appears that not much has changed since Mark Twain's day—at least when it comes to how adults sometimes feel about teenagers.

The truth is, many parents dread the teenage years. But youth expert Joe White, author of the book *What Kids Wish Parents Knew about Parenting,* says it doesn't have to be that way. Believe it or not, according to White, it's even possible to live happily through the teen years! Here are a few practical steps he suggests to make the teen years more positive:

- Listen to your teenagers. Teens must have parents who are eager to listen, slow to speak, and full of understanding—parents who are ready, willing, and open when their kids want to talk.
- Spend time with your teens. Attend their games and concerts; stay up and talk with them after their parties and dates; and take them with you on errands.
- Get to know their friends. Insist that your kids bring their friends home, and begin this when they're young. The friends they

choose will tell you a lot about what your kids are like away from home.
- Set a positive example—with the language you use, the movies you watch, and the way you spend your money. Your example will help your teens make good choices in the face of temptation.
- Establish a connection between privileges your teens can earn—like talking on the phone, driving the family car, going out at night, and receiving an allowance—and proven responsibility.

Last, and perhaps most important, White advises us to pray for our teens. Pray for their ability to stand alone, for their self-image, and for their desire to honor and obey us. Pray for their future spouses, their teachers, coaches, and friends. Sound advice from a man who knows.[1]

BEING A FATHER AND A FRIEND

It was a day Larry would never forget. He was five years old, and his favorite aunt had come for a visit. When she surprised him with a gift of a plastic ball and bat set, he was so excited he immediately ran out to find his father. He found him working in the garage.

"Daddy, Daddy," young Larry shouted, showing his father the new ball and bat. "Would you come out and play ball with me?"

Larry's dad leaned up from the car and stared at his little boy—a long, piercing look that Larry would never forget. "Let's get something straight," he said. "I'm your father, not your friend." Forty years later Larry remembers those chilling words as if they were spoken yesterday.

Men, we have a priceless opportunity to be more than just biological fathers to our sons and daughters. We can also be their best friend. If we will take time out from the things that keep us busy to do something special with our children instead, it will mean the world to them. Our kids grow up with many negative influences. As fathers we have the chance to make a positive difference. But sometimes we "check out" of any intentional, active involvement in our kids' lives.

In his book *Straight Talk,* family psychologist Dr. James Dobson shares a startling statistic from a study of the amount of time the average middle-class father spends with his small children: thirty-seven seconds per day! Far too many dads are out golfing, working on the car, or at the office putting in "a few extra hours." Meanwhile, the next generation is suffering from—among other things—a lack of healthy fathering.

"Be very careful, then, how you live—not as unwise but as wise, making the most of every opportunity, because the days are evil" (Ephesians 5:15-16). The next time you're tempted to give your children the runaround, make a point of giving up your "right" to do what you'd prefer with your spare time. Engage with your kids, and do something they would enjoy. Men, let's be more than fathers to our kids. Let's be friends.[2]

BIKE FATHER, BIKE SON

Ever feel like you can't relate to your son? Try learning to enjoy what he enjoys. Ed Morris, 45, says he likes bike racing with his thirteen-year-old son, Jake, because they both get to participate and root each other on. Jake says he likes racing just because it's fun. Father and son train together two or three days a week on roads and trails near their California home, and some weekends they travel to various race venues to compete. Ed and Jake have different motives for riding bikes, but both love the sport and enjoy the time they spend together.

Sometimes it seems like men do better when they're doing things together. We watch sports, play pickup games of basketball, or jam on guitars. Likewise, we can bond with our sons by hanging out with them. No matter how old our sons are or what they like to do, we can find fun things to do with them.

Men, let's try to find activities we can do with our sons—things that'll be a kick for them and for us. If your son is young, it might be as simple as tossing a Wiffle ball and letting him swing the bat. He may miss every time, but remember, the activity isn't the point—the point is to be together.

As your son grows older, his interests will change. Make sure your interests evolve, too. Learn how to play hacky-sack and video games. Try to boogie board, rollerblade, or whatever your son wants to do.

Your time together doesn't have to be active and athletic either. Perhaps your son is interested in drama—you could help him practice his lines. If he's interested in science, take him to free lectures at the local university, where you both can learn more. If he's interested in music, make concerts in the park a priority. Whether you're seriously interested in these activities or not—this is serious bonding time with your son. When you participate in these activities together, you'll grow closer to him—and conversations will flow out of that relationship.[3]

BOYS NEED ROLE MODELS

Boys are more likely than girls to die before the age of eighteen, are more likely to run afoul of the criminal justice system, and are nine times more likely to be patients in drug and alcohol rehabilitation programs. What can we do to help them?

Vernard Hampton, a substitute teacher in Los Angeles, says that he's amazed by the number of boys he encounters who lack a basic understanding of how to be men. He does what he can to help the boys in his classes. "Even something as simple as learning to shave," he says, "they can't figure out on their own. I'm big on talking to the boys in my classes."

Did you know that about 50 percent of divorced fathers lose all contact with their kids after the divorce? When you consider that more than half of all marriages end in divorce, millions of boys are left without any influence from their father. Boys need role models. Unfortunately, their families are often in chaos.

Each of us men has survived to become who we are, and that alone qualifies us to share our valuable experience with boys who need guidance. These kids are just trying to figure out their identity as men in a world that doesn't give them healthy masculine examples. It doesn't matter whether we have children of our own or not. We need to help these boys who don't have caring men in their lives.

Chances are you know a single mom who is struggling to raise her son. Your family could befriend hers, and you could become a role model to that boy. It might be as simple as showing him how to use a razor or tie a tie. It might be as complicated as giving him advice about girls. At least you could invite the family to your home for a meal and let the boy see a man who has stayed with his family.

Millions of fatherless boys in our country are desperate for help. They need men in their lives. There are plenty of us to go around. So let's find ways to share ourselves with them.[4]

CONSTRUCTING THE
ESSENTIAL FATHER

Hey, dads, a study by the American Psychological Association tells us we're unnecessary to our children's lives! Can you believe that?

It's true. In an article titled "Deconstructing the Essential Father" in the June 1999 issue of *The American Psychologist*, the authors declare that fathers are a financial drain and an obstacle to the nurturing of their children. Professors Carl Auerbach and Louise Silverstein, who readily admit their political bias in favor of family structures not headed by heterosexual, married couples, report that fathers might actually be detrimental to their children's well-being. *Detrimental!*

However, the conclusions of a more recent study shake the foundation of their findings. According to the *Archives of Pediatrics & Adolescent Medicine,* the greater a father's involvement in his children's lives, the better off his children will be.

The researchers of this new study looked specifically at the differences between homes with no father present, homes with an uninvolved father present, and homes in which the father was both present and actively engaged in his children's lives. The researchers found, not surprisingly, that it was not just the father's presence in the home that was essential but also his active involvement in the lives of his children. A father who is active in his children's education, recreation, and spiritual life will benefit their overall well-being. On the contrary, a father who comes home, flops down in his recliner, and ignores his children is not much better than a totally absent father.

So, dads, while some scholars work to deconstruct the essential father, we ought to be in the business of constructing the essential father—which means more than bringing home the paycheck and putting food on the table. Being an essential father means playing an active, not a passive, role in our children's upbringing. It means being involved at their school, at church, and in their extracurricular activities. Dads, these are practical ways to show our children how much we love and care for them.

Professors Auerbach and Silverstein conclude that children would be better off if Dad just got lost. The truth, however, is that the essential role of a father is to build character into the lives of his children. Fathers, let's get involved.[5]

GIRLS NEED THEIR DAD FOR
A POSITIVE SELF-IMAGE

According to New Moon Publishing, 90 percent of the five million Americans who suffer from eating disorders are adolescent and young adult women. By the time girls move from elementary school to high school, only 29 percent are happy with their looks, compared to 60 percent before. And every model that young girls see, admire, and want to be like weighs 23 percent less than the average female.

Dads, if you have young daughters, this is a problem that you will face or are trying to figure out right now. Your little girl is being infected with a new, insidious disease—the perceived need to be thin and beautiful. You may hold one of the most significant keys to helping her create a positive self-image: You are her father. There is no other man in her life who can spend days and months and years showing her why she is one of the most spectacular girls who has ever lived. But, as fathers, we can also destroy the fragile, incredibly delicate spirit growing within our daughters. We have an awesome responsibility. And it's terrifyingly easy to make a mistake that might be hard to fix.

In the face of all that, what can we do to protect our daughters from anorexia, bulimia, and other unnatural obsessions with dieting? We dads need to value our girls for all of their positive characteristics—their charm and grace, their intelligence, their athleticism, their leadership abilities, or whatever it is that makes them who they are. We need to make the extra effort to notice where they are gifted and encourage those gifts. Your little girl needs to know that you think she's beautiful; but even more important than that, she needs to know how valuable and wonderful she is in every way.

We also need to be careful not to be hypocritical, checking out all the women we encounter, reducing them in our mind to little more than objects of beauty and lust. The Bible says that "man looks at the outward appearance, but the Lord looks at the heart" (1 Samuel 16:7). We need to be the face, voice, and heart of God in our girls' lives.

ITIVE

LUNCH WITH YOUR SON

Let me tell you about a father who worked nights but didn't want to lose touch with his ten-year-old son. Every day he traveled to the boy's school and ate lunch with him. That's a nice idea, isn't it? Well, the school administrators didn't see it that way. They didn't mind an occasional visit, but they saw these daily lunches as excessive and unhealthy, and they intervened to stop the father from coming to school.

How unfortunate for a school to send an active, attentive father home. Here is a father who refused to let his job keep him from daily time with his son, yet he was penalized. If the visits were disruptive, I'd understand. But that wasn't the school's claim.

My friends, I believe our society has lost its priorities. You know, every year thousands upon thousands of births occur with no father present. Marriages end, and Dad disappears. Children are growing up without a father in the home, and the results are seen every day at school, where fatherless boys perform much worse than those from two-parent homes. Statistics compiled by the National Fatherhood Initiative point to other detriments experienced by the fatherless. For example, they are far more likely to join gangs and take drugs.

To his credit, the father I told you about didn't give up. He still has lunch with his little boy, but only once a week. I wonder whether those administrators will someday regret their decision. As the years go by, they'll see thousands of boys who don't know their fathers, and they'll remember the man who came to campus every day.

Men, the years go by quickly, don't they? The little boy who sat on your lap and asked you to read a book to him—the child who imitated your every move—is now asking for the car keys. And one day the little girl who called you Daddy and demanded a kiss every morning and a hug every night will bring home a boy whom she calls *honey*. We can't miss the opportunity to enjoy these years. We should take advantage of this time to be close to our children—or grandchildren. We'll never regret time spent with children. Not for a moment.[6]

NEWS MEDIA CELEBRATE
SINGLE FATHERS

Are married fathers going the way of the dinosaur? In an article in *The Weekly Standard,* Dr. David Popenoe highlights some very disturbing information about the state of fatherhood in the United States. It seems that several of our largest newspapers, including the *New York Times,* the *Chicago Tribune,* the *Washington Post,* and the *San Francisco Chronicle,* featured single dads almost exclusively in their 2001 Father's Day coverage. Dr. Popenoe observes that in order to be honored on this holiday, a man had to be either "not married to his child's mother or married but biologically unrelated to his child."

Without a doubt, fathers find themselves in a variety of situations these days, and we should certainly respect those who are facing the challenges of single fatherhood or who are members of blended families. However, Dr. Popenoe rightly notes that singling these men out to the exclusion of others suggests an agenda on the part of newspaper editors. He says, "Any celebration of single dads that goes beyond an entirely appropriate recognition of individuals striving to do the best they can by their kids amounts to a celebration of divorce and other causes of nonmarital child rearing."

In essence, the media are trying to tell us that when it comes to children, single parenthood and cohabitation produce the same results as an environment of married parents. But in light of the overwhelming evidence showing that children are better off being raised by two parents rather than one, the media's celebration of single parenthood seems irresponsible at best.

Men, we must continue to support those who find themselves parenting alone, but we also need to expose the dangers of thinking it doesn't matter whether a child is being raised by one parent or two.

Perhaps you know someone who has fallen for society's lie that unmarried parents can create just as healthy an environment as married parents. Without being preachy, point these misguided friends to the solid research that clearly shows there is no substitute for a married, two-parent environment when it comes to the spiritual well-being and emotional development of children. It's time for us to speak out against this campaign of misinformation.[7]

PARENTS VITAL TO KIDS' SUCCESS IN SCHOOL

Some schools are sending students home with a report card to evaluate their parents' performance. Report cards for moms and dads may sound extreme, but overwhelming evidence points to parents as the single greatest factor in determining their children's academic success.

Although a student's grades are closely tied to things like family income, race, and educational background, many studies have shown that the most accurate predictor of a child's school performance is how well his or her parents have created a home environment that encourages learning.

In other words, if our kids aren't doing as well in school as we think they should, we might need to look in the mirror. The problem is—and this is why some schools are resorting to report cards for parents—many mothers and fathers remain uninvolved in their kids' education.

It has been proven that school performance improves when parents set demanding, yet reasonable, expectations for their children's scholastic achievement. And that's not just the mother's responsibility. It's our job as fathers to contribute to a climate in our homes that values learning and promotes discovery and exploration. For starters, let's turn off the TV and read to our kids when they're young. Most children love to hear stories, and it sends them a strong message about the value of reading.

Let's put a little wear and tear on those library cards, and encourage our kids to read on their own as soon as they're able. And then, let's point them to books that match their interests as they grow up. After all, as is commonly acknowledged, reading is the foundation of all education.

When our kids start school, we should ask them about their school day, praise them when they do well, and encourage and help them to develop discipline and healthy study habits.

Men, what power we have! By taking an avid interest in our children's education, we parents—more than any other people—can help ensure our children's success in school. Let's do it![8]

RESPECT—EARNED AND LEARNED

Can you think of a recent family film in which one or both parents are not missing, stupid, useless, dangerous, helpless, divorced, or dead? Parents in movies are seldom portrayed as very useful, and kids many times have to be the heroes and save the day.

Popular culture does not teach kids to respect their parents. Homer Simpson is more of a clown than a father figure to Bart. Buffy the Vampire Slayer appears almost to live in a world without adults. The kids of *South Park* seem to look at adults as an unnecessary evil on the face of the earth.

Maybe your kids don't watch these shows, and there *are* some shows that have healthier family situations, but many of your kids' friends are influenced by the popular culture—and it's something we have to be aware of as fathers. There is a not-very-subtle lesson being taught—and caught—that parents are not to be trusted. Sadly, many parents indeed fit the stereotype. With so many absentee fathers, a huge number of kids grow up without a dad, and many others grow up living with grandparents. Who suffers? The children.

Despite this bleak cultural trend, the good news revealed in survey after survey is that kids want to be able to rely on their parents. Teenagers are dying to spend time with both Mom and Dad, to talk to them about the confusing questions of life, and to enlist their help to get through tough times.

Even though it may seem like your kids think you are a dinosaur with no useful ideas about the hard questions of life, they want to know that you are there to support and encourage them. And they know that they need your wisdom and experience.

Respect for parents has to be learned in the home because popular culture sure doesn't teach it. Not only do your kids need to learn to respect you, but you, as parents, need to be worthy of their respect. Dads, you need to teach your kids by modeling respect for your wife and by treating your kids with the respect you want in return. It may be the hardest thing you'll ever do, but it will surely be the most rewarding.

Kids & Culture

SHARING YOUR SKILLS WITH KIDS

What would you do with a bunch of kids who stole golf balls from your course? How about teach them to golf? That's what Mike Williams, head pro at the Chester L. Washington Golf Course near South Central Los Angeles decided to do. In the seventeen years that Williams has been teaching kids, he estimates that thousands of youngsters have gone through his junior golf program. Sometimes he's dipped into his own pockets to help pay for equipment. Kids who've been in Williams's program have had their grades improve, and many have won college golf scholarships.

All a kid really needs to enroll is a commitment to learning and a willingness to accept instruction. During his classes Williams stands before two dozen young people and talks like a drill instructor. He teaches them about the patience and the quiet of the game of golf. He teaches them about etiquette and safety. He teaches them about respect. And if any of them don't like it, they can go home. Williams, an African-American, was at work teaching young people about golf long before Tiger Woods began breaking color barriers in the sport. But with Woods's emergence as the game's dominant player, interest in golf has never been higher among minority kids.

Mike Williams has taken his gift and his vocation and applied them to helping kids who are in need. What's stopping us from doing the same? You know, men, all of us can take our skills and make them available to kids. Are you a writer? How about contacting a local tutoring agency and offering your services a couple of hours every week? Are you a machinist? Considering the cutbacks in their metal-shop programs, schools could probably use an expert to come in and help kids learn. Are you a skilled gardener? Perhaps an inner-city program could utilize your talents to teach children something new. Some urban kids have never had the experience of watching something they planted with their own hands flourish under their care.

The things we do and take for granted can be used to teach and inspire kids. Let's take some time to invest in the next generation. We'll learn through our service, and we'll offer kids skills to help ensure a bright future.[9]

ABSTINENCE? HOW DO YOU DEFINE THAT?

What do anal sex, oral sex, and mutual masturbation have in common? Many young people believe these activities qualify as sexual abstinence! A study by the Urban Institute on the sexual practices of fifteen- to nineteen-year-old boys nationwide found that young people are engaging in a variety of sexual behaviors, and many are confused about what constitutes abstinence.

According to the findings, more than one in ten boys had engaged in anal intercourse, half had received oral sex from a girl, and slightly more than a third had performed oral sex on a girl. Researchers, public health experts, and health care workers have found that many young people perceive oral and anal sex as something other than sex—and often even as abstinence.

Men, we're going to have to get more specific when we talk to our children about sex. If we teach abstinence but let them define it for themselves, they're going to flirt with danger sexually. We need to let our kids know that practicing abstinence doesn't give a green light to every act this side of intercourse.

As fathers, we've got to enter into our young people's lives and help them develop a healthy understanding of sex. Yes, having these frank conversations is going to be uncomfortable for everyone, but it's critical that we not shy away from the topic. Even if it's awkward to talk about this stuff, let's try to open the door of communication sensitively with our kids. Let's be purposeful instead of reactive about our kids' sex education.

When we have these discussions, we have to let our kids know that we love them, we care about their well-being, and we want the best for them. We need to tell our kids that we're here for them. This isn't a one-shot conversation either. If we build a bridge of trust, it should pave the way for future conversations.

Fathers, let's not be too busy or too scared to talk to our kids. These conversations will bond us together with our children and could save them from unsafe and immoral sexual practices. When we talk about sex directly and sensitively, we communicate the truth in love.[10]

BREAST ENLARGEMENTS
FOR TEENS?

In England, when Jenna Franklin announced that she would have cosmetic surgery to enlarge her bustline on her sixteenth birthday, it was all over the news. Jenna said that the procedure was necessary to ensure her chances of success in life. Perhaps the worst thing about this whole situation is that her parents not only approve of her decision—they're paying for it!

Call me old-fashioned, but I think there's something terribly wrong here. When our girls start believing that they have to have large breasts in order to succeed in life, things are way out of whack. I'm pleased to know that I'm not alone in opposing this kind of thing. Dr. John Grossman, chairman of the plastic surgery department at Rose Medical Center, says that he doesn't know a "real" plastic surgeon "who would think it's appropriate for a sixteen-year-old to have breast implants."

Jenna, no doubt, is a victim of an advertising and marketing system that uses sex appeal to sell everything from soap to SUVs to self-esteem. When you consider all the busty women who grace the covers of magazines at the supermarket checkout and those who fill our TV and movie screens, it's no wonder that girls like Jenna feel the way they do.

I agree with Dr. Grossman that Jenna's parents are neglecting their parental responsibilities. They're affirming their daughter's over-emphasis on physical beauty as the ultimate measure of worth at a time when any loving and responsible adult would be doing everything he or she could to counteract such lies. It's our job, as parents, to refute the destructive messages our kids get from the media. When our young girls start believing that they must have supermodel looks to succeed in life, it should raise a big red flag.

As responsible fathers, we need to remind our daughters that they're unique and special individuals with eternal value and worth and that it's the inner beauty of the soul that means the most. We need to teach them to love themselves just the way they are. We can do that by accepting our daughters fully ourselves, no matter what their shape or size.[11]

COMBATING NEGATIVE
PEER INFLUENCE

Did you know that middle schoolers are nine times more likely to smoke and five times more likely to drink if they have two or more friends who smoke or drink? I recently came across two studies that drew the same conclusion: Our children are greatly influenced by their peers when it comes to substance abuse.

The first study found that elementary-age kids start out with negative attitudes toward smoking, alcohol, and illegal drugs. But when they hit the middle school years, they take a dramatic turn. Girls are especially vulnerable to peer pressure to start smoking cigarettes, drinking alcohol, and using illegal drugs.

The second study, not surprisingly, found a direct link between early teenage drinking and adult alcoholism. A large number of teenagers who began drinking at an early age ended up with severe drinking problems and personality disorders by the tender age of twenty-four. Depression and drug abuse were also more common among teenage drinkers.

Both studies also agreed on the most important factor for preventing our teenagers from caving in to peer pressure. Any idea what it was? Parental involvement. Both teams of researchers suggested several ways that we can point our kids in the right direction:

- Stay involved in their lives. Know what your kids are doing and who their friends are.
- Have high expectations for your kids. Most children will rise to your expectations when they know that certain behaviors would disappoint you.
- Hold your children in high regard. Listen to them and respect their opinions.

Bruce Simons, one of the researchers, puts it succinctly: "Teens who reported that their parents were highly involved in their lives were about half as likely to smoke or drink as young people who felt their parents were not very involved." Now that's significant!

Dads, let's make sure we're closely involved in our children's lives. Let's not only talk with them but let's listen, too! Let's show them that we value what they think. And let's not underestimate them. Our kids may surprise us by not only meeting our expectations but exceeding them. And with our involvement they can avoid the trap of teenage substance abuse. "The wise in heart are called discerning, and pleasant words promote instruction" (Proverbs 16:21).[12]

FRINGE YOUTH

Since World War II, America has been wondering what to do with its teenagers. With the increased number of families in which both spouses work and an increase in single-parent families, the adult world and the world of adolescents have less in common than ever before. Not only have parents lost the ability to relate to their kids, but their kids are no longer interested in relating to their parents. Over the past several years, teenagers have created their own separate society with the help of marketing firms and the media. Their world runs by a different code than that which governs the adult world, and its members generally hold in contempt all outsiders, including adults and authority figures.

Parents who have tried to be involved in the lives of their children often decide to cut their losses and give up the battle. They end up retreating to the adult world to avoid being alienated from their kids. The result is that many kids, as they move through the ranks of teen society, never learn to relate to others in a responsible manner.

Parents need to understand the antiparent messages their children receive from the youth culture and not be intimidated! Take a lesson from Cassie Bernal's parents, who chose not to retreat but instead helped their daughter turn her life around before her untimely death at Columbine High School. Children have just as great a need

for authority in their lives now as they ever have—it's just that their culture is telling them something different.

The foremost principle in this process of saving kids from their own culture is love. What is happening to our kids should break our heart, and our love for them should motivate us to reach out to them, even when it is difficult and painful.

Dads—and moms—sometime this week, take your son or daughter out for breakfast and a one-on-one talk. Express your love and care, and affirm his or her value. It'll be the best investment of time you'll make this week. Let's not let the youth culture dictate the way we raise our kids.

HEALTHY FAMILY LIFE
PROMOTES ABSTINENCE

Cultivating a healthy marriage will keep you and your wife happier. And it could also help your kids avoid premarital sex.

It's no secret that teens are more sexually active today than ever before. Everywhere you look, sex is being aggressively marketed to the younger generation. Is it any wonder that so many teens are practicing what is preached to them by their culture? And yet, out of this hormonally charged battle, an interesting statistic has emerged. A study conducted by the University of Chicago shows that even though teens are by and large more sexually active than ever before, those who come from intact families are much more likely to practice abstinence until marriage. In fact, the research indicates that the best demographic indicator for whether a teen is likely to abstain from sex is the condition of his or her parents' marriage.

Men, the entertainment industry doesn't care whether or not you want your kids to remain sexually pure until marriage. As long as there is an audience, it will continue to pump out material that can lure young minds into a world of heartache, unplanned pregnancy, sexually transmitted disease, and more. But if coming from a healthy home environment makes teens more likely to embrace abstinence, then let's strive to make our home as affirming and appealing as possible. Let's resolve now to ensure that our relationship with our wife is worthy of our kids' respect and admiration.

There's no end to the ways we can model a positive marriage for our kids. Do nice things for your wife "just because." Buy her flowers. Take her out to dinner. And when conflict arises, learn to handle each situation with patience, understanding, and humility. Your kids will learn more from casually observing the way you interact with your wife on a daily basis than they ever could from a thousand stern lectures about the pitfalls of sexual promiscuity.

In the end, there are so many reasons for us to cultivate a stronger relationship with our wife. But the fact that our kids are watching—and will benefit from our example—is one of the most compelling reasons of all.[13]

KIDS—GLUTTONS FOR MEDIA

I t's obvious that the media play a huge role in the lives of our kids.
The question is, should we be doing anything about it? Sixty-one
percent of parents reportedly have decided to let their kids make
their own choices about their media intake. For many kids, the media
wind up playing too influential a role in their lives. Two authors of recent books, psychiatrist Stanley Greenspan and Kay Hymowitz, agree
that kids and the media spend too much time together.

A survey by the Kaiser Family Foundation revealed that children
ages two through eighteen spend nearly five-and-a-half hours a day
outside of school with some type of media. Of that amount, almost
three hours are spent watching television. In 1979 just 6 percent of
children had a television in their bedroom; today 77 percent do.

One problem with media saturation is that it can isolate children.
Kids can't have a two-way conversation with the television, and
cyberchats don't develop communication skills. Kids who become
addicted to media often give up time playing with friends in order to
spend time at the computer or watch TV.

To keep kids focused on reality, parents need to take control. We
need to evaluate how big a role the media play in the lives of our
kids. One sure way to find out whether media saturation is a problem
for your family is to try going without it for a while. This may sound

extreme, but the withdrawal symptoms your family suffers will indicate how addicted you've become.

After your "media fast," discuss the experience with your family and determine reasonable time constraints for your media intake. For example, Dr. Greenspan believes that an hour of TV a day is enough. What's best for your family? Also, what's a reasonable amount of time to devote to the Internet, and under what conditions should it be employed?

The media can be a great enhancement to our kids' lives, offering educational and entertainment value—but not if they rule their lives. Let's keep a leash on the media so that we can continue to be the number one influence on our kids.[14]

SAFE DRUG USE FOR KIDS?

You've probably heard about Brittney Chambers, the young woman who died after she took the drug Ecstasy on her sixteenth birthday. She purchased the pill in a school bathroom—and now her school is promoting the idea of "safe drug use"!

Besieged by accusations of rampant drug abuse among the student body and feeling the need to do something, high school officials responded with an absurd measure. They brought in a so-called expert to give a thirty-minute presentation on the safe use of club drugs! Taking a "nonjudgmental approach" to combat drug abuse, Emmanuel Sferios, executive director of a group called DanceSafe, told the students, "We neither condemn nor encourage drug use . . . but we recognize that, like premarital sex, young people are going to do it."

I don't know about you, but I find that approach both disturbing and irresponsible. Is the notion of "safe drug use" really the message our kids need to hear today? Brittney's fatal decision proves that even club drugs like Ecstasy can be deadly. Her story alone should demonstrate that "safe drug use" is a lie.

Our society doesn't suggest that "kids are going to smoke anyway" so young people should "smoke safely." We recognize the inherent contradiction in that message. The same logic applies to "safe drug use."

Men, we need to set high standards for our kids' behavior, establishing clear standards of right and wrong, and letting them know that we expect them to avoid things like smoking, sex, and drugs—regardless of what other kids are doing or what may be considered "cool" or "politically correct." Our children need to be encouraged to make good character choices. We must talk to them about these issues, communicate our expectations, and express our confidence in their ability to exercise good judgment and self-control.

"Just say no" may seem like a simplistic and out-of-date approach to teen drug use, and maybe it is, but we ought to be absolutely clear that drug use is simply bad for our kids. If that's being judgmental, so be it. Our kids' lives are at stake.[15]

TATTOOED TEENS

attoos used to be reserved for sailors and tough-looking guys on motorcycles. Nowadays we see them on professional athletes and actors—everything from barbed wire to butterflies to elaborate designs covering large patches of skin—and they have become increasingly popular among young people. Some would say that tattoos are simply a harmless expression of individuality or just the latest way for a younger generation to distinguish itself from its predecessors. So, what's the big deal? Well, a study conducted by the University of Rochester in New York provided strong evidence that a tattoo may be a visible clue that a teenager is headed in the wrong direction. The survey showed that tattooed teens were almost four times as likely as their peers to have had sex, 2.7 times as likely to be gang members, and about twice as likely to abuse drugs, alcohol, or cigarettes or to have taken part in a recent fight.

I would suggest that, although there are exceptions, a tattoo is often a sign of teenage alienation. When teens become involved in negative behaviors, it's usually because they feel that their parents either don't care or aren't genuinely interested in their lives.

Dads, if your teenager has obtained a tattoo, you probably ought to sit down with him or her for a few heart-to-heart talks. If you're upset, take a while to cool down and choose a time when you, your wife, and your child can calmly discuss what's going on in his or her life. You might want to begin by sharing the results of this New York study and expressing your concern. It might turn out to have been a decision based simply on peer pressure. But if you suspect a more serious problem, you may have to intervene to prevent further damage.

The best way to prevent this kind of "surprise" from occurring is to maintain a close relationship with our children from the time they're young. Open communication with our kids will help them to feel loved and understood, alleviating feelings of alienation and allowing us to address issues like tattoos before, not after, they happen.[16]

TELLING THE TRUTH ABOUT SEX

According to researchers at the State University of New York at Albany, teens who think their parents condone their use of birth control are far more likely to lose their virginity than those kids whose parents have tried to impress upon them a message of sexual abstinence.

Parents have a huge opportunity to tell their kids the truth about abstinence and share with them the need to remain celibate until marriage. In a survey conducted by the National Campaign to Prevent Teen Pregnancy, 58 percent of teens said that sexual activity for high school–age youth is not acceptable, even if precautions are taken against pregnancy and sexually transmitted diseases.

Be encouraged! These are kids coming to good conclusions! Contrary to popular thought, 87 percent said they don't think it's embarrassing for teens to admit they're virgins. Still, every father needs to do his best to impart the message that abstinence is okay. Nearly every teen questioned (93 percent) agreed that it's important for adolescents to be given a strong message that they should abstain. Our kids need our support and encouragement.

Unfortunately, movies, music, television, and video games blatantly promote unhindered sexual activity. And sadly, more than one-third of teens said they haven't had a single helpful conversation with their parents on the subject. Dads, this is where we must step up to the plate.

The reality is that adolescents are most likely to adopt their parents' attitudes about sexuality if Mom and Dad take the time to discuss sex and related topics. But don't try to get by with a "once-in-a-lifetime" lecture. Kids don't respond well when we simply drop the bomb and try to get on to another topic without allowing discussions to evolve.

Believe me, it's a hard topic. And sometimes we may feel as if we'd do better talking to a brick wall. But it's up to us to plant the seed, no matter how uncomfortable we may feel. We owe it to our children to teach them the truth. Even if we've lived a less-than-perfect life, we can use our mistakes to show them the pain involved in wrong decisions.

Try it, men. I guarantee that even your feeblest effort will top anything society has to offer.[17]

Marriage

ARE YOU COMMITTED?

We've all seen it happen: A coach or athlete gets a better job offer from another team, his current contract goes out the window, and he leaves his former team behind, whistling all the way to the bank. It's gotten to the point that we really don't expect sports figures to abide by their contracts anymore. The trouble is, it seems that many people treat marriage the same way.

In his book *Coaching Your Kids in the Game of Life,* the late Ricky Birdsong points to lack of commitment as a problem that not only affects sports but also devastates marriages and families. Birdsong, who was the head basketball coach at Northwestern University before he was murdered, cites the situation faced by professional assistant coaches. The temptation to "jump ship" can be intense, especially at the end of a successful season when teams are shopping around for talent—even while their current teams need them for the play-offs.

Of course, losing a coach during the play-offs can devastate a team's chances of winning. Successful sports teams, like successful families, need stable, consistent leadership that only comes from unshakable commitments—from leaders who decide to stay together for the good of the team.

Birdsong explains that the Latin root of the word *decide* literally means "to cut off all other possibilities." In other words, we make a decision to keep promises, honor contracts, and maintain commitments, regardless of circumstance.

Here's the question: Have you made an unshakable commitment to your wife and family? On your wedding day, you probably promised to love, honor, and cherish your wife "till death do us part." Did you mean it, or when difficult times come are you tempted to look for greener pastures?

No one pretends that it's easy to keep commitments. At times, Birdsong admits, it just comes down to "hanging in there." He also exhorts men to find friends who will encourage them to work harder on their relationships during tough times rather than take the easy way out.

As men, we need to decide to honor our marriage vows, cutting off all other possibilities. Consistently choosing to love our wife should be the only option we consider.[18]

MARRIAGE: THE FIRST TWO YEARS

A few years ago I came across an interesting piece of research about the importance of the first two years in determining whether a marriage will last or fail. Not surprisingly, couples who experienced disillusionment or had negative feelings toward their spouse within two months of their wedding were likely to divorce in less than two years. But here's what surprised me: The couples who were the most romantic and loving at the beginning had trouble going the distance as well. Their marriages tended to last only about seven years on average. Their life together started out like a roaring fire, but they burned out quickly. Those who maintained positive feelings toward each other and who approached marriage as a marathon, not a sprint, had the best chance of success.

Men, how can we help our marriages to "go the distance"? If you're single but in a serious relationship or thinking of marriage, the first essential step is to receive strong premarital counseling to help you learn more about your prospective partner and to master the communication skills needed to make your marriage last.

"Husbands, love your wives, just as Christ loved the church and gave himself up for her" (Ephesians 5:25). After you're married, it's important to do the little things on a daily basis to show your wife how much you love her. You don't have to shower her with flowers and diamonds every day. Instead, you need to listen to her and share your heart with her so you can build a strong base of emotional intimacy. That's not easy for most men, but it's essential if you want your relationship to grow.

Tonight, instead of turning on the television and tuning out your wife, sit down over a cup of coffee or tea and spend some quality time one-on-one. Perhaps you can read a book together—one that will bring insight to your marriage. Or maybe you can set up a surprise date and take your wife out for a special dinner and evening. Whatever you choose to do, look for ways to affirm your wife. Your encouragement will keep your marriage strong long after the first two years are over.[19]

A GAME PLAN FOR MARRIAGE

No football team starts a game without a strategy for success. No marriage should either. Getting premarital counseling will provide you and your fiancée with a strategy to survive all the ups and downs that will come your way.

A while back, one hundred scholars, religious leaders, and civic leaders met in Denver to discuss what could be done to stem the high divorce rate and strengthen marriages in our country. Out of this meeting came an agreement titled "The Marriage Movement: A Statement of Principles." This pact called for the reconsideration of no-fault divorce laws, encourages marriage over cohabitation, and advocates "covenant" marriages, which make obtaining a divorce more difficult. But perhaps the most important provision called for counselors to be more proactive in helping couples work out their problems *before* they tie the knot, not after. The participants agreed that all couples disagree from time to time, but those couples who have learned proper communication skills are able to weather those storms and emerge with an even stronger union.

Unfortunately, many couples race off to the altar without giving a thought to premarital counseling. Diane Sollee, director of the Coalition of Marriage, Family, and Couples Education, speaking about how many young couples prepare for marriage, says, "Right now, we're sending couples out onto the football field and not telling them the rules." The result? The marriage is over before it's even halftime, leaving a trail of broken hearts and devastated children.

Premarital counseling will help you develop a winning game plan for your marriage. If you are thinking of getting married, or getting engaged, I strongly urge you to go to training camp before the big game. If you're getting married at a church, ask whether it offers premarital counseling—and sign up.

If the church does not offer such a program or you're getting married elsewhere, I suggest that you contact a local marriage and family counselor and make an appointment. The time, money, and effort you spend before you say "I do" will be an important investment for the success of your marriage after the ceremony is over.[20]

HAPPY MARRIAGES VS. UNHAPPY MARRIAGES

Do you sometimes feel as if your marriage is an uphill climb? The difference between happy marriages and unhappy marriages is not as great as you may think. University of Minnesota researcher David Olson examined answers from a nationwide couples inventory used by more than forty-five thousand counselors. Two areas that seemed to have a profound effect on a couple's satisfaction were communication and spirituality. Couples who have trouble communicating and don't share common spiritual beliefs have a much harder time forming a successful marriage than those who practice good communication skills and are in tune spiritually.

Olson advises: "Pay attention to your relationship like you were dating. And praise your partner for the positive things. After marriage we tend to focus on what we don't like—on what bothers us about a partner." So often, after the dating days are over and reality sets in, we end up focusing on what we perceive to be our spouse's faults rather than her many positive attributes. In the process, a wall the size of Mt. Everest can go up between a husband and wife. No one likes to be criticized, and eventually the person being torn down will start to shut off communication rather than be hurt repeatedly. It is our role as the husband to make our wife feel honored, respected, and special.

One of the ways that a husband can show his wife that she is special is to pray with her. Prayer creates an emotional intimacy and a bond that brings couples together. It allows husbands and wives to get beyond small talk and to express their deepest feelings. Husbands, you should initiate times of prayer with your wife. Take her hand and ask her how she's doing and how you can pray for her. Share your thoughts and feelings as well. Then give thanks for your marriage and the blessing your spouse is to you. In the process, you and your wife will grow closer together and develop a bond that can weather whatever storms may come your way.[21]

HOLLYWOOD MARRIAGE OFF TO A ROCKY START

A one-million-dollar-per-year flat fee, plus a five-million-dollar penalty if the deal goes sour. This sounds like a big-money business proposition, but it's actually a marriage contract!

When two big-name Hollywood stars were married in 2000, it was hardly a storybook romance. Before tying the knot, they hammered out a complex prenuptial agreement that must have kept their lawyers working overtime. Most notably, the groom—who admitted to having an affair with his former wife's best friend—agreed to pay his new bride a five-million-dollar "fling fine" should he ever cheat on her.

Now don't get me wrong. I believe in new beginnings, and I wish this famous couple every happiness as they endeavor to forge a healthy relationship while managing busy careers and facing constant media attention. But their prenuptial agreement is characteristic of too many "what's in it for me?" marriages today.

Newlyweds no longer look forward to experiencing life's peaks and valleys as a team. Instead, the marriage relationship is too often tainted by suspicion and distrust. Can any couple really expect to build a successful union on such a shaky foundation? Life together requires a readiness that doesn't come from binding documents and legal stipulations. If the signing parties really need a legal agreement in order to "protect" themselves and their property, they shouldn't get married in the first place!

Men, we need to learn to be servants and strive to love unconditionally. Mutual trust, commitment, and selfless love are all prerequisites for a successful marriage. They aren't optional. If you're getting married, make sure that you and your fiancée have talked openly and honestly about questions and expectations before moving forward with the relationship.

For those of us already married, regardless of how long, we must remind ourselves to put the needs of our marriage above our own—and to do so on a daily basis. No matter what stage of life we're in, marriage is no place for a "me first" mentality. It's about love, sacrifice, and mutual servanthood.[22]

THE NIGHT-SHIFT BLUES

When Dad gets home around 6 p.m., he finds a familiar note on the fridge: *Gone to work. Dinner can be heated in the microwave. The kids need showers. I'll be home around midnight.*

Two-income couples have become a way of life in America. Unless we know otherwise, we might naturally assume that both parents are working daytime jobs and are home nights and weekends. Unfortunately, for many families that isn't the case, and they are paying a price for it. A recent study done at the University of Maryland found that families with parents working different shifts have a much greater chance of divorce than those families with only one parent working or both working the same hours. Why is this? Well, families need time together. Couples need time together. Families start to drift apart when job responsibilities keep them from spending significant time together for days and weeks on end. As the author of the study says, "If indeed social interaction among family members builds greater bonds, communication, and caring, we would expect that the more time spouses have with each other, the more likely they are to develop strong commitments."

For some families, two jobs are needed simply to put food on the table and clothes on their children's backs. That is reality. However, sometimes the sacrifices we make—working two jobs and odd hours—

are not the sacrifices our family really needs. If we're compromising time together with our wife or kids only to keep up with the Joneses in material possessions, maybe we need to revisit our priorities.

If you and your spouse both have to work, I encourage you to try to schedule your jobs so you are both home at the same time. If you're only working so you can afford that new SUV or a huge home, I encourage you to reexamine your family budget and find a way to get by on one income. Our relationships will benefit from the kinds of sacrifice that best serve our family commitments.[23]

YOUR WIFE AND YOUR BLOOD PRESSURE

Your heart may no longer skip a beat when you're around her, but your blood pressure probably goes down!

Most men once had an intense, loving relationship with the woman they married. Unfortunately, for many those days are over, and they now live more as roommates than lovers. Still, most of us could think of plenty of good reasons to spend time with our wife. She's someone we've promised to love, cherish, and honor—forsaking all others. We should want to spend time with her, period. But it's an interesting fact—an intriguing bonus—that when we do spend time with our wife, our physiological health is better, too.

Did you know that men have lower blood pressure when they are with their wife than when they are doing other activities? It's true. Several studies have noted the connection between the emotional health of our marriages and our physical health. A recent study sponsored by the National Heart, Lung, and Blood Institute noted that a man's blood pressure goes down when he's with his wife more than in any other circumstance—more than when interacting with friends, even more than when he's alone. And get this: Men who reported an overall "less satisfying" relationship with their wife *still* experienced lower blood pressure in her presence. In addition, when meeting or talking to someone else, having their wife present actually had a calming effect on their blood pressure.

This new study is noteworthy, but obviously men should have motivation to spend time with their wife already—including nurturing a healthy marriage. It's simply a bonus that our health is improved as well. Perhaps a wise man named Solomon was on to something, some three thousand years ago, when he wrote this exhortation: "Enjoy life with your wife" (Ecclesiastes 9:9; see also Proverbs 5:18).

Make it a point today to spend some time with your wife. Ask her (if you don't already know) what she likes spending time doing with you, then do it. If necessary, schedule time together in place of some other activity. Relax and let your blood pressure go down—both figuratively and literally![24]

YOUR WIFE . . . YOUR BEST FRIEND?

She's your lover, your companion, your fiercest supporter, and your most honest critic. She's your wife. But is she your best friend? A study by a group of University of Washington psychologists found that the key to a successful marriage is friendship. This may seem like a no-brainer, but it's easier said than done. In a one-hour interview, the researchers asked couples a series of open-ended questions, more to observe the process of their interactions than for the precision of their answers. The study found that the way a couple interacts when discussing issues is central to understanding how healthy their relationship is. Do both partners value the other's views and opinions? Do they treat one another with respect? Do they listen?

Couples who have a strong bond speak in one voice. Each partner knows the perspectives of the other and keeps his or her partner's wants, needs, and priorities in perspective when forming opinions.

If we want our marriage to be healthy, we need to develop a true friendship with our wife. One gauge to measure the level of our friendship with our wife is how highly we esteem her and her thoughts and views. Are we willing to grow and change in ways that connect us to our wife's heart? Or do we expect our wife to change who she is in order to get along with us? When we honestly try to change our own perspective, we show our wife that we value her enough to relate to her.

Have you spent any time in the last week building your friendship with your wife? I'm not talking about watching a football game together but doing things that she enjoys. Write your wife a note telling her how her special character complements yours and makes you a better man. Share with your wife the ways she has changed you for the better.

If we husbands do these things, our wives are bound to take notice! Take a chance on developing your friendship with your wife. You might shock her, but your marriage will be strengthened as your friendship develops.

PECTIVE

Singles & Relationships

THE COHABITATION MYTH

Men and women living together before marriage was once rare. Now it happens more often than not! But new research shows that instead of helping a future marriage, cohabitation actually hurts it.

Many men choose to live with their girlfriend to enjoy the sexual benefits of marriage without the formal commitment. They convince their girlfriend that they will marry in the future, and sometimes they do.

Brad was one such guy who told his girlfriend that they might get married when he asked her to move in with him. But really, he didn't have any intention of marrying her. When his girlfriend continued to talk about wedding plans, Brad found himself in a difficult situation. The relationship was tormented by tension and distrust for months until it finally ended in disaster. Brad's girlfriend found out the truth and left. Both of them were devastated and Brad had additional guilt from hurting a woman he'd cared about.

Pamela J. Smock, a sociologist at the University of Michigan Institute for Social Research, the world's largest academic survey and research organization, recently led a study about cohabitation. Her findings are significant. First, the percentage of marriages preceded by cohabitation rose from about 10 percent in 1965 to more than 50 percent by 1994. In other words, living together before marriage is now more common than not living together before marriage. Also, marriages that were preceded by cohabitation were more likely to end in divorce than those in which couples had not lived together before marriage.

Men, a relationship that lasts is built on 100 percent sold-out trust and 100 percent sold-out commitment. The first step toward achieving this is to be honest. Tell the truth about your intentions in a relationship. And if you truly value the relationship, you need to practice honesty and self-control.

When we realize the damage that's done through cohabitation, we will begin to understand the importance of the institution of marriage. Marriage is more than just a "piece of paper." It's a lifetime journey based on trust.[25]

DATING VIOLENCE

Young love; sure, it hurts. But a new study revealed that for students between the ages of thirteen and eighteen, dating is too often a setting for physical abuse—primarily against girls. The study found that one-third of all teenagers have experienced physical violence in a dating relationship. Many girls reported being punched or forced into sexual situations against their will. Almost half the girls said they sustained bruises and injuries requiring medical attention.

Violence against boys is less common and often happens as girls resist unwanted sexual pressure and other aggression from their male dates. Of the boys who were pinched, slapped, scratched, or kicked, more than half later laughed about the incident, saying they weren't hurt at all.

Interestingly, both boys and girls blamed dating violence on the boys. One out of five boys attributed their aggression to their own jealousy. And more than one-third of the boys claimed to have been drunk. Worse yet was the news that fewer than 3 percent of these violent incidents were reported to an adult outside the family and only 6 percent to parents.

What has happened to our society? We can blame the influence of violence in movies and on television or video games or pornography or even just eroding moral values—all of which contribute to the problem. But my question is, "What can we, as fathers, do about it?" I suggest that we must take an active role in preparing our sons to treat women right.

The first step is to treat our own wife and daughters with love and respect. And we should expect the same from our sons in their interactions with girls. Let's watch for language that demeans women. If our boys are picking up cruel stereotypes from their friends, we should gently but firmly correct them.

We can coach our sons on their relationships with girls. We must teach them to keep their hands to themselves and to focus on talking with their female friends and learning about the girls they spend time with. Who will teach our sons that women aren't sex objects and aren't to be overtaken violently if not their dads? Let's teach our sons to value other men's daughters the way we'd want someone else's son to value ours.[26]

FLEE TEMPTATION ISLAND

The folks at Fox TV had an idea for people in serious relationships: Toy with the temptation of infidelity. On the "reality" show *Temptation Island,* four unmarried but seriously involved couples and thirty single tempters and temptresses tested the waters of temptation. The couples were split up and sent to explore the single world. After two weeks they had to decide between possible new love interests and their old flame. *Temptation Island* made a game out of fidelity and temptation!

Men, it's not likely we'll visit a real Temptation Island, but temptation is something we deal with every day. The problem with temptation is that it gets us thinking with our libido instead of our logic. Temptation doesn't encourage coherent decisions about a relationship; it seductively tells us to give up control.

I remember a story I heard about a millionaire who was looking to hire a driver for his limousine. He asked each of three candidates the same question: "If we're driving on a narrow mountain road, close to a cliff, how close could you come to the edge without sending the car into the ravine?"

The first driver said, "I can have the tires of the limo within three feet of that cliff and still keep you totally safe." The second driver said, "I'm such an expert driver that I can have the edge of the tires hanging over the cliff and still keep you safe!"

The third driver looked the millionaire in the eye and said, "I'm such a good driver that I'm going to stay as far away from the edge of that cliff as possible—and maybe even take a different road." The third driver got the job.

Men, let's give ourselves a reality check! The only thing to do when tempted is to flee. Run away. Vamoose. Get outta Dodge. We can't toy with temptation, enjoy it, or even tolerate it.

Temptation undermines fidelity, and whether we're married or hoping to be married one day, we must practice fidelity. When we flee temptation, we're able to think clearly about our relationships and give them the best chance to thrive.

LIVING TOGETHER

Whether it's due to skepticism about marriage, a fear of commitment, or pure lust, many men and women choose to live together apart from marriage. All cohabiting couples have their reasons. They tell themselves that a marriage certificate is only a piece of paper and that they don't need to justify their love for each other. Or they believe that living together will enable them to test the strength of their relationship. It's an arrangement that seems to offer all the benefits of marriage without the restrictions. It's maximum pleasure with minimum problems—a deep relationship combined with personal freedom. Remaining together is based on choice rather than legal compulsion.

Sounds good, doesn't it? But these couples are deluding themselves, especially if what they want is a long-lasting relationship. According to sociologist Pamela Smock, most couples who live together either marry or break up within eighteen months. Only one in six are still living together after three years, and one in ten are with each other after five years. Those who do marry are far more likely to end up divorced. Smock says, "When you look at the data, it becomes difficult to maintain the position that marriage isn't better." Clearly, it is.

Other experts have found that cohabitation seems to affect those involved by making them more individualistic and less relationship-oriented. In fact, studies show that married couples who don't live together before they tie the knot are happier, more faithful to each other, and better off financially than those who live together first.

It may sound old-fashioned, but it's obvious that marriage—not "shacking up"—is still the best option for couples who truly want a satisfying and long-lasting relationship. As one marriage expert says, even if couples see living together as a trial marriage, "it should really be [called] a trial divorce."

Men, if you're truly in love with a woman, the best recipe for a lasting, satisfying, and happy relationship is to get to know her thoroughly as a person, keep your own quarters, and save sexual intimacy for marriage.[27]

MAN MARRIES TV

It was probably just a matter of time, but it has finally happened. A man has married his TV! According to a news source in England, Australian Mitch Hallen, with the blessing of a priest, wed a Sony widescreen television at a ceremony in his living room attended by a dozen of his friends. Vowing to "love, honor, and obey" his new "bride," Hallen placed a gold wedding ring on top of his television set to match the one he placed on his finger. The priest then pronounced the couple man and wife. It wasn't reported whether the groom kissed his new spouse.

Apparently, after two divorces, Hallen had decided to give up on women. "My TV gives me countless hours of pleasure without fussing, fighting, or backchat," he said. "So I feel I'm better off marrying it rather than another woman."

Who can argue with that kind of logic? Television offers an endless stream of entertainment choices for virtually every taste twenty-four hours a day. With remote control over a "mate," whose only purpose in life is to make him happy, Hallen considers his television set "the best companion I've ever had."

We laugh at this, as well we should, but I think we have to admit that there's a little of Mitch Hallen in all of us. The truth is, we men tend to love our TVs, often "tuning out" our wife and family for hours on end. And let's be honest: Our remote control gives us such a sense of being in charge that many of us would rather die than give it up. The trouble is, it's all too easy for television to take the place of communication and meaningful relationships at home. Real relationships involve hard work, risk, and limited control. Relating to human beings usually involves differences of opinion, the potential for rejection, and the inevitability of conflict. Nevertheless, the rewards of meaningful relationships far outweigh the risks. For all the benefits of TV, nothing can replace a loving wife, not to mention children. Let's commit ourselves to our relationships, to loving and serving our wife and family, and to working through our problems. Isn't that what marriage is really all about?[28]

SEARCHING FOR A SOUL MATE

Are you seeking a soul mate? If so, you've bought into Hollywood's destructive notion of love.

A survey conducted by David Popenoe of Rutgers University indicated that many young, single adults are on a quest to find an idealized "soul mate" who will meet their every physical and emotional need. Unfortunately, in their search these young people, mostly in their twenties, seemed willing to disregard traditional notions of marriage and family. Sixty-two percent thought it was okay for a single woman to have a child outside of marriage; 44 percent had cohabited; and only 16 percent believed that the main purpose for getting married was to raise a family.

The Family Research Council observed that many young Americans seem to be shopping for a mate as they would a car, with live-in partners "traded in" for newer models. The FRC put much of the blame on television programs like *Seinfeld, Frasier, Dharma and Greg, Drew Carey,* and *Sex in the City*—not to mention *Friends*. According to columnist Don Feder, programs like these consistently convey the message that "singleness is swell; sex can be separated from marriage; a woman without a career is pathetic; career—measured by power and money—is all-important; and personal gratification is life's highest goal."

The truth is, there's no such thing as a "perfect mate." We're all flawed, and we all fail to meet expectations at times. Beyond that, living together increases a couple's chances of divorce, as does the idea that your supposed "soul mate" may be someone other than your spouse—especially after the romantic fires have burned down or when problems arise in a marriage.

Lasting marriages are based on unconditional love and unshakable commitment—not on finding the perfect mate—and the healthiest families are still the "traditional" variety: a husband, a wife, and children. "The evidence has become quite strong that children's prospects are most promising when they are wanted and are raised by both of their parents in a low-conflict marriage," says Carol Emig of the group Child Trends.

Men, let's rear our children to have a realistic view of romance and a healthy view of marriage. Let's love our wife and kids unconditionally and keep our commitment to "love, honor, and cherish" our wife "till death do us part."[29]

THE STIGMA OF SINGLENESS

More and more Americans are plagued with what many see as a depression-inducing and seemingly incurable disease. They're single!

John is thirty-three years old, handsome, charming, and intelligent, but he's never been married. We could make all kinds of assumptions about his singleness. *I wonder if he has some flaw keeping him single. Maybe it's something in his personality that makes him unattractive to women. He probably wishes he were married. Maybe he'd like to be set up with my friend Judy. Or it could be that John is a closet homosexual.*

Ever notice how many stereotypes we have of the single men and women we know? We often make up reasons for their singleness—reasons that are almost always negative and likely have no bearing on reality. Despite the fact that the ranks of single people have skyrocketed over the last three decades, many psychologists agree there's a social stigma attached to being single. This view is supported by a study in which 143 people were asked for their impressions of various "bank executives" named Lee: a single woman, a married woman, a single man, and a married man. Participants' evaluations were significantly more negative of the single characters.

Let's be clear. Singleness is not a disease to be cured. Singles don't necessarily have a reason for being single. There is no universal age to get married. And pity may not be the appropriate response to singleness. Not all singles are unhappy being unmarried. Not all singles feel incomplete or lonely. Some single people live very full lives. But this doesn't mean they don't have struggles just like the rest of us.

Those of us who are married need to spend time with singles, invite them to dinner, include them in our family activities. In other words, we need to treat them like human beings and not loners or matchmaking projects. Singles and married couples need to learn about life from each other's perspective.

Let's recognize and then eliminate the biases we have toward single people. When we do, we'll start operating based on reality instead of stereotypes.[30]

WAITING IS WORTH IT

He had waited a long time for this moment—thirty-seven years to be exact. Greg had seen all of his friends make the trip down the aisle and sometimes wondered if his turn would ever come. Now it had, and the day was even more special because he knew that he could look his bride straight in the eye and tell her he had saved himself only for her.

It had not been easy, and at times he had been sorely tempted. Many of his friends had fallen off the abstinence bandwagon, and Greg had often been mocked because of his virginity, but he had stayed the course. Remaining sexually pure is one of the hardest tests we can face as men. We are bombarded daily by sexual messages in the media, by peer pressure, and by our own sexual nature to give in to temptation and have premarital sex. But there are good reasons to remain sexually abstinent. From a practical viewpoint alone, it's one way to guard against sexually transmitted diseases, pregnancy, and emotional devastation.

Sexual intimacy has no place outside marriage. So how can we keep ourselves sexually pure? First of all, we can monitor what we allow ourselves to be exposed to. Pornography, for instance, even in its mildest forms, not only devalues women, it also stimulates us sexually. Let's use plain old common sense and avoid the temptations of unwise situations. Let's set up boundaries at the beginning of our relationships, before it's too late, and then let's exercise the strength and determination to stick to our convictions. Let's start our relationships with women on a solid foundation of respect, consensus, and trust.

If you have already been involved sexually outside of marriage, make a vow to yourself to refrain from similar decisions in the future. It won't be easy. And I strongly suggest enlisting the help of some good friends to keep you accountable to these new standards. The payoff will be worth it.

Perhaps you hope to get married one day. If you maintain your purity, on that day you'll be able to stand before your bride and know that you have respected her enough to put your concern for that committed relationship before your own desires.

Character

THE ANGELS OF CASCO, MAINE

Shayne and Corey Earley were born with a rare genetic condition that practically guarantees they'll never see their fifth birthday. The condition destroys the fatty covering that insulates the nerve fibers in their brain. As a result, neither can swallow or move, and both are almost completely blind. They have to be fed intravenously and must be aspirated frequently to help them breathe. Their parents, Lawrence and Yvette, wake up every morning wondering whether their three-year-old boys will live to see another day.

"We say our good-byes every day," Lawrence laments, "just because we don't know [if they're going to make it through another day]."

As in the case of most birth defects, the cost of caring for Shayne and Corey has been astronomical. Before long, the Earleys found almost all of their income going to the boys' care and were unable to pay their bills and their mortgage. It was then that the people of Casco, Maine, came to their rescue.

As neighbors learned of the Earleys' plight, they started to pitch in and help out. One resident, Mike Vaughn, dealt with their creditors and got them off the Earleys' backs. A local pizza shop donated free meals to those who volunteered to help and also served as a collection center for donations for the family. Yet another resident organized fund-raising events for the Earleys, and a local garage fixed their cars for free.

Yvette Earley was amazed. "They just rose to the occasion and knocked our socks off. All I can say is 'thank you.'"

"Love your neighbor as yourself" (Luke 10:27). Men, our neighborhoods extend far past the streets we live on. Let's keep our eyes open for someone who may be in need. It could be a homeless person, a lonely senior citizen struggling to get by, or a young person who has trouble fitting in. Let's teach our kids the value of helping someone out as well. Serve in a soup kitchen as a family, take meals to a shut-in, invite a lonely person over for dinner, or just put an arm around a hurting child. Let's use the example of the people of Casco, Maine, as an inspiration to extend a hand of friendship to someone in need.[31]

DRIVING WHILE AGGRESSIVE

If there's anything worse than running out of gas on the freeway, it's having someone lean on his horn, pull up too close behind you, and make a gesture that says, "I don't care what your problem is, just get out of my way." Road rage has become a familiar term. It occurs when a driver gets so angry that he loses all control. Instead of pulling over and cooling down, he'll run another car off the road, yank someone out of the driver's seat, and punch him . . . or worse.

What we don't often hear about, though, is "aggressive driving"—when someone operates a motor vehicle in a way that endangers people or property. Aggressive driving includes cutting off other vehicles, speeding, running red lights, or passing without having enough space. Although these actions may not seem as serious as road rage, more people are likely to engage in this kind of recklessness. Since 1990, thirteen thousand people have been injured or killed in crashes caused by aggressive driving.

A recent survey found that more than 60 percent of drivers consider unsafe driving—including speeding—to be a personal threat. A full 67 percent said they had been "frightened by another driver" within the past year.

Security guards are subjected to a series of questions before being issued a firearm for their shift. This procedure allows a supervisor to objectively assess a guard's stress level or identify danger signs that could affect his decision to use the weapon. We ought to apply the same standards to our driving. Think of a car as a massive weapon under our control. Before cranking the ignition, we need to ask ourselves if we're facing unusual personal difficulties, stress, or exhaustion. If so, we should stay home or call a friend or a cab.

When you see an aggressive driver in the next lane, here are a few tips. Stay as calm as possible, and completely avoid eye contact. Get out of the way, and let the nut drive on by. Just pull over, and call the Department of Public Safety or police to report the reckless driving. We all need to keep our emotions in check when getting behind the wheel of a car. Otherwise, anything could happen.[32]

OUR GREATEST GIFTS

In 1998 Clint Hallam received an amazing gift. Three years later he threw it away.

While in prison in New Zealand, Hallam lost his hand to a chain saw. Not too long after, he was given an incredible opportunity—the chance to receive the world's first hand transplant, donated from the victim of a motorcycle accident. The transplant was a success, and Hallam had a new hand. All he had to do was take some medicine every day and continue physiotherapy.

Somehow the chance to have two good hands instead of one didn't impress Hallam. One day at a time, he made little decisions not to take care of himself, and over the next couple of years, he let his new hand die. Finally, surgeons had to remove it and throw it away.

Hallam made some really poor decisions—but many of us make similar decisions without even realizing it. We decide to work late or all day Saturday. We forget our kids' band concerts and miss their soccer games. We can't seem to find time for breakfast with our wife, or we neglect to surprise her occasionally with a bunch of flowers. It's easy to waste the gift of a loving wife. The gift of children. The gift of health. It can happen one drink, one concert, or one bunch of forgotten flowers at a time.

Maybe you remember being a young boy and wanting some

wonderful present for Christmas and getting that present. Then a few days or weeks later, it was out in the rain rusting or lost down in the park, and you'd forgotten about it. We can't do that with our loved ones. They are the most precious gifts we've ever been given. Each day they need to be loved and cherished. We don't have days to waste. Somebody gave Clint Hallam a hand. He wasted it. Men, we need to take the time to cherish our gifts.[33]

HE CHOSE DEATH

It was July 1941. The sirens of Auschwitz blared, and guards raised their rifles. A captive had escaped. Nazi rules dictated that if one man escaped from the camp, ten innocent men would be starved to death as punishment. So hours after the escape, the six hundred tattered men of Block 14-A gathered in the courtyard so that the Nazi commander could select ten to die in an underground starvation cell known as the Hunger Bunker.

The Nazi officer methodically examined each man, either calling him forward for extermination or passing him by. Father Maximilian Kolbe, a battered but noble priest, stood among the unkempt group. Ignored by the commander, he was granted life.

At the age of forty-seven, Kolbe had been captured and taken to Auschwitz for his lifelong faith and ministry. The Nazis specifically targeted priests for extra torture and abuse. Father Kolbe slaved at the most difficult work assignments and withstood merciless beatings. But even in his suffering, he served his comrades, offering encouragement and prayers in the night. Fellow prisoners knew him to be peaceful, humble, and compassionate.

As the ten condemned men were herded toward the Hunger Bunker, one cried out, "My family, please . . . my children!" The prison guards sneered, and the survivors watched with mixed emotions.

Suddenly a disturbance arose within the ranks of the men. Father Kolbe stepped forward. Hat in hand, he calmly approached the Nazi commander and said, "I wish to make a request, please. I want to die in place of this prisoner." Kolbe pointed to the sobbing man who had pleaded for his children.

The Nazi commander was shocked but considered the inquiry, then granted the priest's request. The two men switched places. The sobbing father, now stunned, rejoined the spared prisoners of Block 14-A. He was never able to express his gratitude to Father Kolbe, who was led away to suffer in the Hunger Bunker. While there, Father Kolbe bravely comforted and cheered the other dying prisoners, leading them in song for their final days of life. Two long weeks later, Father Maximilian Kolbe died for a man he barely knew. It was the greatest possible expression of love.[34]

THE NEED TO FORGIVE

I once read a story about a man with an interesting name: Yatin Dave. Dave was about thirty years old when his body was found in a sleeping bag by the side of U.S. Highway 50 in Colorado. Actually, it wasn't his body; it was his skeletal remains. He had died of hypothermia about a year earlier, and his corpse had lain untouched for a year before it was discovered by a prison work crew. By then, there wasn't much left of Dave's body.

The story in the paper was tragically short. It took an investigator a month to find anybody who remembered Dave—and longer still to find a relative. When she contacted Dave's dad, it was only to find that he and his son had had a fight and had not been in contact for three years. Three years!

There's a harsh lesson for all of us to learn from this. Disagreements and arguments are unavoidable between any two people, especially between people who love each other, but we can't neglect to forgive each other and ask for forgiveness. Men can be unusually bad about this. Many times we're so proud and convinced that we're right that we refuse to see our own fault—or more important, to see that our relationships are what count in life, not being right. Here's a father who was so angry about something that he lost his son until it was too late.

RGIVE

Forgiving others and asking forgiveness for ourselves is both completely simple and incredibly difficult. But we need to put our relationships with those we love and care for first. We can allow ourselves a little bit of time to be angry, but "do not let the sun go down while you are still angry" (Ephesians 4:26).

When we've had a disagreement, we can show true character by walking into the room and apologizing honestly and humbly. Pride is not a virtue. Humility is. Pride can cost us valuable relationships, but humility costs us only pride. Men of character know how to apologize and how to forgive.[35]

PRAISING AND ENCOURAGING OTHERS

I recently picked up a new habit from a gentleman I know named Miles McPherson. Miles is a former NFL player for the San Diego Chargers who's now an author and speaker to thousands of young people and parents each year. Miles teaches a practice that has stuck with me. It's simple. Ask those with whom you come in contact this question: "Do you know what I like about you?" Then follow up the question by saying something positive about the person. It's actually an easy habit to develop, and the goodwill that comes from accentuating the positive is mysteriously contagious. I say, "You know what I like about you?" to my wife, Lyndi, every day. And it's fun because I never run out of new things to say.

My friend and colleague Dr. Dave Wardell is also a world-class encourager. In his book *Daily Disciples,* he writes, "Communicate positively rather than focusing on the negative; be on the lookout for ways to express appreciation toward others. 'Major' in praising people."[36]

Have you ever tried to share encouraging words with those you interact with each day? Does your wife know what you like about her? Do your children? Coworkers? Parents? It's not that hard to find at least one thing you like about other people. And when you do, don't keep it to yourself, tell them.

As we try to keep up with the ever-demanding pace of life in our society, we risk growing distant, sometimes even from those closest to us. People around us—even our family—may not know how much we care about and appreciate them. Men, we can lead by being encouragers to those with whom we spend time, praising their positive attributes. In so doing, we give honor where honor is due. Try asking, "You know what I like about you?" to the first few people you see after reading this message, and then follow it up by sharing something positive. Be sure to remember your family. Do it until it becomes a habit.

OURAGE

THE MEANING OF IMPORTANCE

José Morena spends his workdays sweeping trash, wiping toilets, and scrubbing floors as a custodian at Lincoln Elementary School in Oxnard, California. He's been on the job for fourteen years. And though he excels at his work, it isn't what he's known for at the school.

During recess, Morena's a quarterback. With his ring of keys jangling from his belt loop, he throws spirals to pint-sized receivers. His presence on the field makes the friendly games more fun and prevents spats, according to the students. He does the same on the basketball court.

The kids on the playground light up when asked about Morena: "I've known José for a really long time, and he's always been there for me. He's someone you can talk to, and he understands," says ten-year-old Amber Castillo.

Morena also helps the teachers in the classroom. Because he's bilingual, he can translate between teachers and parents. He also stands in for teachers when they have to leave their classrooms. Morena has two daughters of his own, but he also acts as a father figure to many of the students, particularly boys, who don't have fathers at home.

Some people think that you have to have an impressive job or powerful position to have an impact on people's lives. But José Morena is living proof that you don't have to be the man in charge to be important. Being important is about serving others. It's about playing with kids, even when you don't have to. Importance is about being man enough for kids to consider you a role model.

Men, we've got to ask ourselves what we're living for. Do we equate importance with having the most powerful sounding job title and the biggest paycheck? Do we disdain tasks that we think are beneath us?

Let's go the extra mile at work, even when it means we won't be recognized or compensated. Let's do the menial work without grumbling and complaining. And maybe, just maybe, we'll be the kind of man who's important to every person he encounters. Take a look at José Morena. This elementary school janitor just might be the most important man on campus. Let's allow ourselves to shine like a light no matter what our position.[37]

TICKET TO READ

Randy Murphy drove for thirty years without a driver's license. Why didn't he have a license? That's simple. He couldn't read, so he couldn't take the test. He was like a lot of folks in this country—millions of people—who can't read but somehow get by.

Murphy might have gone on that way for the rest of his life if he hadn't turned up his car radio one day and been stopped by Officer Mark Taylor for blaring his music. Taylor wanted to know why Murphy didn't have a license. When he found out that Murphy couldn't read, Officer Taylor could have just written a ticket and been done with it. That would've been easy. Instead, he showed the type of character that every man should show. He offered to help Murphy learn to read. For three months they studied together. Then it took Murphy six times to pass the driver's license test. But with Taylor's help and encouragement, he finally passed. Today, the two men have become friends and continue to read together.

It is easy to skip a lot of chances we have as men to make a difference. Some of them are small, and some are bigger, but they usually present themselves without warning, without giving us time to prepare ourselves to say yes or no—or sometimes even to think about them. Consequently, we must develop the necessary character so that when those moments of opportunity arrive, there's no hesitation between seeing the need and acting.

Someone once said that you can't change the entire world, but you can change the world for one person. Maybe, for some of us, changing the world means taking a moment to care for a homeless person, to treat him or her in a humane way. It might be as simple as befriending a neighbor who is of a different race. It might be looking out for the fatherless kids we come across. Whatever it is, each of us can change the world, one person at a time. Over the years I've missed some chances to make a difference. I pray that you and I won't miss too many more.[38]

The Internet & Pornography

COMPUTER COMPULSION

What is found in most American homes and is causing all sorts of problems for its owners in their work, personal, and social lives?

If your answer is the home computer, you're right! As computers become an integral part of the home, many Americans are becoming chained to the mouse and are spending less time with family and friends. Wives are going to bed alone as their husbands spend hour after hour surfing the Internet. Old friends are forsaken for chats with anonymous individuals.

Instead of fostering a so-called global community, computers are causing people to become more socially isolated, according to a study done by Stanford University. Dr. Norman Nie, the principal researcher, says, "The more hours people use the Internet, the less time they spend with real human beings." Another study showed that people who spend an excessive amount of time glued to the computer screen start to show signs of personality disorders, such as moodiness, anxiety attacks, and substance abuse. The people monitored in this study reported that their computer use had interfered with family, friends, work, and school. When they tried to cut back on their computer time, they experienced withdrawal symptoms and became anxious.

As Dr. Nie puts it, "If I go home at 6:30 in the evening and spend the whole time sending e-mail, I wake up the next morning and I still haven't talked to my wife or kids or friends. When you spend your time on the Internet, you don't hear a human voice, and you never get a hug."

The computer and Internet can be wonderful tools if used properly and in moderation. Many people have reported how they have renewed old friendships via e-mail. The vast information available on the Internet makes it valuable as a research tool as well. However, the computer and the Internet can also be tools of destruction when used excessively or if they draw individuals into areas such as on-line pornography. Men, we cannot allow ourselves to fall into this tangled web.

Put your family and friends first, and use the computer and the Internet only as you would use any other tool—to help you get a job done. There is no substitute for human relationships, especially for those within your own home.[39]

MAKE A COVENANT WITH YOUR EYES

When it comes to sex, men are visually stimulated. With pornography easily available on the Internet, and scantily clad women everywhere—from TV and movies, to billboards, to the newspaper—it's hard for us to avoid looking, even if we don't want to.

The prevailing attitude among men is that "it doesn't hurt to look." I strongly disagree. And so does Fred Stoeker, coauthor of the book *Every Man's Battle: Winning the War on Sexual Temptation One Victory at a Time.* According to Stoeker, when we allow ourselves to find sexual gratification in anyone but our wife, we do damage to our marriage. "Most men are drawing a good bit of their sexual gratification from the environment surrounding them through their eyes." That violates our vows to "love, honor, and cherish" our wife, and it's a subtle form of unfaithfulness.

The answer given in *Every Man's Battle*, taken from the Old Testament character Job, is to make a covenant with our eyes. As part of a defense of his character, Job said that he'd made a covenant with his eyes not to lust after young women (see Job 31:1). A covenant could be called a deal or a contract.

To fulfill his own "covenant," Stoeker identified his areas of greatest temptation, including female joggers in tight nylon shorts, lingerie ads, billboards of scantily clad women, beer-and-bikini commercials, movies rated PG-13 or higher, and women with low-cut or tight blouses. For those sights that cannot be avoided, he says, "You must build a reflex action by training your eyes to bounce away from the sexual immediately, like the jerk of a hand from a hot stove."

Men, we're tempted daily to let our eyes stray. Let's take Fred Stoeker's advice and make a list of the five things that most tempt us visually—and devise a strategy to avoid them. And let's teach our eyes to "bounce away" from those temptations we can't avoid. Stoeker reports that as a result of making a covenant with his eyes, his desire for his wife "jumped off the scale," leading to a stronger marriage.[40]

GAME ADDICTION

For the better part of nine months, Dan Gilbert lost his wife to an Internet game. Each day she retreated to her computer in the basement, surfacing only to sleep and grab a quick bite to eat. Her computer log showed she played an average of sixty-five hours a week. "It was like we were in different worlds," Dan said. "She didn't do much of anything except play that game."

Lori was playing one of the new types of Internet games—computer-generated fantasy worlds where thousands of players can talk and adventure together. Unfortunately, the design of the games, which encourages players to spend months and even years playing, has drawn some players into spending dozens of hours a week immersed in a virtual world while the real world rushes past.

David Turner, a fireman in Texas, found the world of on-line games a relaxing and predictable change of pace from his hectic real life. "It was an escape," he said. He made friends on-line and was admired for all his game-playing skills. But after two years of playing, Turner, a father of three who was often on-line for up to eight hours a day, began to realize how little time he was spending with his family.

It's not so hard to understand the desire to escape from reality and live in a fantasy world. But just because we hide from reality doesn't mean it goes away. Not only is it out there waiting for us, but most times it has gotten worse because we have been hiding from it.

The average person spends three hours weekly on the Internet. Internet addicts average nearly twenty hours per week. In addition, the typical American spends almost as much time watching TV as working—well over thirty hours per week.

It's not that we shouldn't have some time to ourselves for the things we enjoy. But if we compare the time we spend entertaining ourselves to the time we spend with those we love, my guess is it will be clear that we need to change our priorities for the sake of our marriage and family.[41]

HUGH HEFNER WAY

It used to be that the naming of highways, bridges, and streets was reserved for people who had made a positive contribution to a community. In Chicago that tradition has been undermined.

In 2000 the Chicago City Council voted to honor Hugh Hefner, the founder of *Playboy* magazine, by naming a street after him. They said that it was their way of thanking Hefner for keeping his Playboy headquarters in the city. In acknowledging this honor, his daughter, Christie, called her father "the quintessential American success story." But there is a dark side to Hefner's "success story." His empire has been built on portraying women as sex objects.

When women are depicted in this manner, their humanity is stripped away, and the message to men is that women are only to be valued for their physical attractiveness. What a devastating lie! *Playboy* has also served as the gateway for many men to enter the world of hard-core pornography, which eventually leads them down the path to destruction.

To those who knew Bob Crane, the star of the old TV show *Hogan's Heroes,* he was an upstanding citizen and a devoted family man. But after exposure to soft-core porn such as *Playboy,* he was hooked and eventually needed more explicit pornography and riskier sexual experiences to fuel his addiction. What did it cost him? Two marriages, his children, and finally, in 1978, his life.

In contrast, several years ago celebrities such as former San Francisco Giants pitcher Dave Dravecky were featured in an ad campaign that carried a simple slogan: Real Men Don't Use Porn. Those five short words are all you need to say.

If you struggle with sexual addiction of any kind, we want you to get the help you need to be set free. I encourage you to visit our friends at Mastering Life Ministries (www.masteringlife.org).

Pornography is addictive and destructive, not only to ourselves, but to those we love. When we reject pornography, we show our wife that we honor and value her, and we keep our heart and mind pure. The men of Chicago may not be able to reject Hugh Hefner Way, but we can reject Hefner's message and embrace Dave Dravecky's instead. Be a real man. Don't use porn.[42]

MEN AGAINST THE MACHINE

The lure of the Internet has been compared to the pull of alcoholism, drug addiction, and compulsive gambling. Internet addiction is insidious and a very real threat to our families. Unchecked, it can have devastating effects on a family man.

Some guys will even destroy their marriage, fail at work, and become hooked on criminal activities by spending too much time on the Web. In the United States the problem has already reached epidemic proportions, and the number of "netaholics" continues to rise as more homes and companies jump on-line with the latest technology.

Cyberjunkies use the Web to escape the bumps and bruises of the real world. They lose sleep, money, and friends because they're always on-line. Often the tie to the machine pushes aside opportunities to nurture and care for loved ones. Being hooked to your mouse doesn't help your love life.

Ask yourself a few questions: Are my wife and children coming in a distant second and third to the cyberbeast? Do I find myself irritated whenever someone from the real world dares to interrupt my Internet wanderings? Is my life enhanced by time in cyberspace? Or am I coming away with feelings of shame and a sense of loss over hours wasted and gone forever? Am I lying about who I am on the Net?

Here's a remedy: Take a week off from the machine. Go cold turkey. Turn it off, and don't touch it or go near it. Then see how you re-spond. Can you take it? Are you burning to log on?

Listen to those around you, especially your wife, when she tells you she's tired of looking at the back of your head. Set realistic time limits when surfing the Web. Maybe you can come up with a way to spend some of that newly discovered free time with your wife! And now more than ever, your kids need your undivided attention. Be-lieve me, your family will appreciate the attention. And, unlike your wife and kids, the Internet won't even know you're gone.[43]

PORN ON THE INTERNET

Technology has been good to us. It helps us fight disease. It helps us feed the hungry. It helps us defend ourselves as a nation. But technology has also created a monster that seems untamable. It's everywhere, it's easy to get to, and it's anonymous. It's pornography on the Internet. When you sit in front of your computer and tap into the Internet, nobody knows you. Nobody sees you. And it seems that everybody is offering you a free, anonymous "peek."

If you had an overwhelming desire to walk into an adult bookstore, you probably wouldn't. There's too much at risk. People you know could see you. But with the Internet, there's no one to hold you accountable. Those most susceptible are young boys. Their hormones are at a lifetime high, and they don't have to be eighteen or older to view porn on the Internet—they just have to say they are.

What the Internet is doing is creating a generation that has seen more pornography than any other—by far. Putting pornography on the Internet is like delivering alcohol to an alcoholic, every day, free of charge, and without anyone seeing the drop-off.

One night in 1993, while Ken VanHyning was surfing porn sites, it was as if he saw the face of his own daughter superimposed on his computer screen. Suddenly, the anonymity was gone. The images were personal. He was horrified at what he had become—a porn addict.

He confessed his addiction to a friend and to his wife, and they agreed to hold him accountable. It has taken time and effort to rebuild a relationship of trust between Ken and his wife, but now their relationship is better than ever, and he is freed from the burden of living with an untamable monster.

If you have become a victim of Internet pornography, I implore you to fight it—run from it. Have your wife or a friend install protective software *and* put in the password. If you're struggling with sexual addiction, start by being honest with yourself—courageously honest. Then confess your problem to someone you know who will keep you accountable. Don't give up hope! You can overcome this.

PORNOGRAPHY LITE

Have you ever noticed that a busty model is staring you in the face from a magazine cover every time you pass a newsstand? There's a new breed of men's magazines, like *Maxim* and *FHM,* that isn't technically pornography but might as well be. The *Maxim* cover includes suggestive titles such as "Score at Will," "How to Take Pictures of Your Girlfriend," "How to Spot a Nymphomaniac," "Touch Her Right Here," and "More Sex! More Girls!" The titles change from issue to issue, but the main topic is always sex, and the content is basically the same.

Men, if we're committed to sexual purity, we must consider our standards. We can't just say we'll read anything as long as it's not porn. We must define and determine the standard of sexual purity we're striving to maintain. Stephen Arterburn and Fred Stoeker, authors of the book *Every Man's Battle,* challenge a common notion about sexual purity. They wonder if men are trying to be "merely excellent" in their level of purity instead of being obedient to a standard that doesn't accept any impure thoughts. If we're holding ourselves to a purity standard of "excellence," we might check out some "pornography lite" at the newsstand and figure we're doing okay. After all, it's not like we're looking at *Hustler.* But men, if we're striving for obedience to a standard of 100 percent sexual purity, it's clear that these magazines can't be accepted.

What if we were to politely stop once a day to ask the grocery store manager or newsstand clerk to please not display the sleazy men's magazines in an open place? If millions of men expressed that they'd rather not see "pornography lite," it would make a difference.

We want to settle for nothing less than absolute obedience when it comes to sexual purity. This obedience will pay off. We'll have a healthier sexuality, we'll have increased desire for our spouse, and we won't be guilty of exploiting women with our eyes.[44]

SAFER SURFING ON THE NET

According to *U.S. News & World Report,* there are more than forty thousand Internet porn sites, many of which have aggressive marketing strategies to increase their exposure, so to speak. *Plugged In* magazine reports that two-thirds of children ages two to eighteen have computers at home and 45 percent have Internet access. Although the Internet is a tremendous resource for learning and communication, it can easily become a nasty houseguest if it provides access to pornography. Fortunately, there are steps we can take to protect our families.

Many "family friendly" Internet providers control the smut. The most common solution is known as a "filter," a feature that distinguishes between appropriate and inappropriate Web content. Filters can be quite diverse. Some services monitor which sites a user can access. Others focus on the ability to control the amount of time a user spends browsing. Still others regulate the kind of personal information kids can transmit on-line.

Whether you're hooking up a home computer to the Web for the first time or considering switching your service provider to take advantage of new filtering technologies, two Web sites can help. Focus on the Family maintains a directory of more than fifty services at www.family.org. Also, GetNetWise.com, a site produced by several commercial and charitable groups, provides an interactive database that will direct you to the service that best meets your needs.

As parents, we need to keep in mind that no matter what electronic precautions we employ, we still need to be aware of what our kids are viewing on-line. One way to monitor our kids' Internet usage is to install the computer in a busy room, like the kitchen or the family room. That way, kids will get used to being on-line in a populated area, frequented by parents who care about the sites that influence them.

Let's keep the Internet under control and see that it benefits our family instead of harming it.[45]

Sanctity of Life

ABORTED FATHERHOOD

Steve and Sue had been married for two years, and they had just found out that Sue was pregnant with their first child. When Steve relayed the news to his mother and father, they were elated.

"Congratulations, *Dad,*" Steve's father said to him with a proud tone. "This is great. I'm finally going to be a grandpa." He patted him on the back. "Way to go, Son."

Steve smiled, but he couldn't shake the unsettled feeling he had inside. *Why don't I feel happier?* he wondered. His mind instantly took him back four years earlier to a time when he was in college. He and his girlfriend had conceived a child, but they decided they weren't ready. An abortion followed. Then the two of them drifted apart. At the time, Steve told himself it was all for the best. Still, something had quietly haunted him through the years. Now he couldn't stop thinking about the child he'd aborted.

The hidden shame of being a man with an aborted child in his past is a feeling that far too many men know firsthand. Although the postabortion trauma experienced by women is well documented, little attention has been paid to the devastation of men. In a 2001 book called *Fatherhood Aborted,* authors David Hazard and the late Guy Condon dared to expose this hidden torment for men.

Men with abortions in their past not only suffer from unresolved guilt like Steve's, but often their lives fall into violence, addiction, avoidance, isolation, and other negative effects. *Fatherhood Aborted* is one of the few resources that isn't afraid to discuss this issue—and in the process it offers hope, healing, and a pathway to truly restored manhood.

With more than forty million abortions performed since 1973, chances are that any group of men—whether at work, at a sporting event, or even at church—includes a man with an abortion in his past. Perhaps you know someone living with this secret. Perhaps that man is you.

Men, you can find hope. A key first step is facing the truth and taking responsibility. When you do this, you can begin to find healing from the past pain caused by an abortion. Be encouraged. Today you can stop acting like a fugitive and find true healing.[46]

ABORTION'S EFFECT ON GENIUS

Jazz great Louis Armstrong and comedian Tim Allen came from troubled backgrounds. Would the world really be better if they had been aborted?

A recent scholarly report put forth a controversial social proposition. It said that legalized abortion contributed overwhelmingly to a sharp drop in crime. The thesis of the study was "a difficult home environment leads to an increased risk of criminal activity." Therefore, the study said, abortions eliminated children who were unwanted and thereby lowered criminal activity.

John W. Whitehead, the founder of the Rutherford Institute, believes—and I agree—that it would be tragic if we concluded from this study that abortion is a formula for a safer, more livable society. What no study can measure, and what we'll never know, are the benefits that society has lost because of abortion. For example, how many geniuses have been aborted? How many people who could have offered this world their leadership, scientific discoveries, or artistic beauty have been lost to abortion?

Louis Armstrong and Tim Allen are two men who've made contributions to our society. Yet both men had troubled pasts. Allen spent time in jail, and Armstrong came from a troubled and abusive home. At some time in their lives, these two men really struggled, but it would have been absolutely wrong for them to have been aborted.

Abortion isn't a solution to anything. Whitehead says that the answer isn't more abortions but taking better care of people who are hurting. We need more compassion. We need to create a world where children are cared for. That's the real solution for both crime and abortion.

Men, what are we doing to be involved in kids' lives? Let's volunteer for and give money to programs that work with needy kids. There are many opportunities to care for kids—it just takes us making it happen.

Another thing we can do is support agencies like your local crisis pregnancy center, which gives mothers an alternative to abortion. Let's value life by making the effort to treasure all children. When we do, we'll not only make our country a safer and better place for kids to be raised, we may just keep future lives from being aborted.[47]

DISPOSABLE CHILDREN

ebi Farris runs a cemetery for babies whose parents abandoned them, leaving them to die. She says, "These children are human beings and valuable, and we've got to stop throwing them away like they are expendable." As she walks past the small graves, Debi recites a litany of heartbreaking stories: "There's a little boy [who] was about a week old [who] was found by a homeless man looking for food. . . . There's a little boy named Daniel [who] was found in a sewage treatment plant. . . . There's another little boy they estimated [to have been] about two weeks old [when] he was put in a trash can. . . ."

These stories of abandonment and death are tragic, but abandonment can take many forms. Equally tragic are the stories of children who've been emotionally and financially abandoned by their fathers after they were born. Hardly a day goes by without another story about a child whose father has done nothing more than impregnate the mother, only to walk away from any responsibility, never honoring his parental and financial obligations. In fact, nearly two million fathers a year fail to pay a dime of child support. But a child is much more than just another mouth to feed or a hindrance to our independence. Raising a child is one of the most honorable and rewarding responsibilities life offers. We cannot treat our kids as though they're something to be disposed of or ignored.

RABLE

Men, we need to embrace our role as a father, not flee from it. Our children need us—all of us, not just bits and pieces here and there. This means we must put other things aside and stop to listen to our children when they want to talk to us. It means we make personal sacrifices that put their needs above our own. It means we're present at the important events in their lives. We don't just look at the pictures after the fact. And if you're divorced, it means honoring your financial and parental obligations.

Most of all, it means that we're devoted to our children and we make them a priority. We're their fathers. That just comes with the job.[48]

ABORTION'S DOUBLE STANDARD

Does a woman's right to choose take away a father's ability to protect his own child?

Charles was taken by surprise when a one-night stand resulted in Mary's pregnancy. He knew that he was responsible, and it was his instinctive desire, as a father, to provide for his unborn baby. When Mary insisted on an abortion, Charles pleaded against it; but in the end he was powerless, and Mary went through with the procedure.

The decision devastated Charles. Although this abortion took place nearly twenty years ago, Charles remains single, has a consuming distrust of women, and has been wracked with guilt and shame for the death of his child.

When it comes to abortion, men face a double standard. "Men [are] told, 'It's her body, her choice,' so they should turn off their emotions," says Bradley Mattes, executive director of Life Issues Institute, which counsels men after abortions. "But if she gives birth, they're told to be good fathers and take care of the child. . . . It's emotional gymnastics that men are totally incapable of."

This double standard confuses our nation's concept of fatherhood, and it's the cause of incredible suffering for potential fathers who have had their offspring aborted. Mattes knows that the guilt and grief from an abortion decision can be tenacious and cannot be willed away. And statistics tell us that there are millions of men suffering every year because of an abortion decision.

Self-disclosure can help to heal unfinished business because it allows men to acknowledge the pain. The question is, do men have the courage it takes to seek healing? If you, or someone you know, need this kind of healing, please call Life Issues Institute's Counseling Referral Program at (513) 729-3600.

Men, the road to healing is close at hand. It is possible to work through the trauma of abortion and move forward in life. With time, I hope that men and women who find themselves in this difficult situation will come to the realization that abortion is not a solution at all.[49]

NUMBING THE PAIN

Be careful what you say and do around that expectant mom. Her baby can hear you and could be learning from you, too. Studies have shown that after infants are born, they are able to recognize music and other stimulus they experienced in the womb. Researchers at the University Hospital in Maastricht, The Netherlands, recently measured memory in the womb using a technique called habituation in which a child in utero is subjected to various vibrations and acoustics. These Dutch scientists discovered that babies *in the womb* have at least a ten-minute short-term memory and a minimum of a twenty-four-hour long-term recall.

But that's not all. Research has made it equally clear that these unseen little ones can also feel pain. Vivette Glover, a leading British physician, in calling for anesthesia to be used during abortions, said, "I am pro-choice, but one should not muddle the two. One thinks about how one is doing [an abortion] in the most pain-free way."

It seems there is no longer an argument about whether or not a child in the womb is indeed a child. Now that we realize a child can remember the strains of Brahm's "Lullaby" played before he was born, the debate is about how to make the killing of a child less painful.

But there's another significant question. How can we convince a woman that giving a child a chance at life is worth a season of inconvenience and anxiety in her own life?

Men, we are often at a loss in discussing abortion issues for fear we'll be called controlling, intolerant, or uncaring. We can undermine those charges by showing that we want to help women facing an unexpected pregnancy. How? We can donate some cash or some time; with our wife we can wallpaper a new nursery or paint a faded room for a single mom. Together we can offer genuine empathy for a hurting woman who may be feeling more lonely and confused than ever before.

Crisis pregnancy centers are also in need of practical, real-world experience and assistance. Let's use our hands—and our financial resources—to touch real people in pain; and perhaps we'll have an opportunity to save another little life in the process.[50]

"JANE ROE" IS PRO-LIFE

Forty million abortions later, Jane Roe has changed her mind. In her book *Won by Love,* Norma McCorvey, the "Jane Roe" of *Roe v. Wade,* exposes the lies of the abortion industry. According to McCorvey, who once worked for an abortion clinic, the counseling given to women by the abortionist, rather than informing them of their options and possible side effects, went something like this: "You want an abortion? You sign here. I give abortion."

It wasn't concern for the woman that drove the process, it was simply money. "As long as she had the money," says McCorvey, "any woman could get an abortion at our clinic, provided she was willing to sign a waiver."

McCorvey could never escape the reality that abortion involves a human life. She continues, "You see the body parts, you hear the women's cries, and you can't keep lying to yourself." In fact, most abortion clinic workers use drugs or alcohol to deaden the dehumanizing effects their work has on them. "You're guilty and you know it," writes McCorvey.

Abortion has been marketed as a safe and easy solution to an unwanted pregnancy—a harmless choice to remove a blob of tissue. The truth is, abortion is neither safe nor easy. Every year thousands of women experience serious complications, and some even die from the procedure. Beyond that are emotional consequences, including guilt, depression, suicide, and difficulty establishing loving relationships—even with their own children.

And for every woman who has had an abortion, there's at least one man involved. Studies have shown that most women wouldn't consider abortion if the father of the baby would stand by her through the pregnancy.

Men, we cannot allow convenience to excuse anything that damages, puts at risk, or, worse, terminates innocent life. It's never right for a man to act so irresponsibly. If you've bought into the lie that abortion is an acceptable alternative, I would encourage you to read *Won by Love*. Norma McCorvey's story provides powerful evidence that opposing abortion and upholding the sanctity of human life is always the right thing to do.[51]

UNWANTED CHILDREN

The day after he opened his Christmas presents, a severely handicapped ten-year-old boy was abandoned at a local hospital with a note reading: "We can no longer care for him." How's that for a merry Christmas?

The citizens of Rockland, Delaware, were stunned when they heard this story. It was easy to assume that the cost was too high. Then the news came that the boy's parents were quite wealthy. Neighbors said the pair seemed to care very much for their youngster, who had cerebral palsy. They took him horseback riding regularly. They took him to movies and out to dinner. They were consumed by his needs. Then, on a cold day in December, something snapped, and all their efforts were overshadowed by one horrifying act that made headlines nationwide.

With time we may learn new details of the decision they made, and we'll still not fully understand it. The factors are multifaceted and complex, and may have accumulated over time. Our culture's perception of children may have played a role here. Laws continue to diminish parental rights. Two-parent homes are deemed unimportant. And in the few two-parent homes that remain, often both parents work, leaving day-care workers to rear the children.

Our priorities as a nation are mixed up. When most families say they just can't afford to have one parent work, what they usually mean is, they can't do it and have all the *things* they want. A standard of living—a lifestyle—has taken precedence over our children.

The parents who abandoned their child in the hospital were very busy. The boy's need for attention clearly detracted from their lives. They could argue that he siphoned their resources—that he robbed them of their chance to really live their own lives. Do you recognize that argument? It's the rallying cry of a generation that is self-absorbed.

Instead, we need to uplift the value of young people. We need to promote the traditional family. Let's demonstrate that sacrifices for the next generation reap satisfaction that no monetary success can touch.

Business Ethics

DESK RAGE IGNITES TEMPERS

Corporate America's latest epidemic is here, and it threatens even the most congenial of workplaces. I'm talking about "desk rage." In a recent survey, nearly one-third of the respondents admitted to yelling at coworkers. Sixty-five percent said workplace stress is at least occasionally a problem for them. Work had driven 23 percent of the respondents to occasional tears, and 34 percent blamed their jobs for lack of sleep. Some passive-aggressive workers said that they even sabotage office equipment to vindicate their workplace suffering.

Stress on the job isn't new, but experts say it has gotten worse. For one thing, layoffs have lessened job security among workers. And these days cell phones and e-mail act as electronic leashes, never allowing employees an escape from their jobs. Luckily, there are several ways we can manage desk rage and its effects.

Don't ignore the symptoms. If a coworker drop-kicks a trash can, his action just might be a cry for help. It may be time for you to chat with him, rather than assume that everything will be all right.

Practice healthy conflict resolution. If you can't leap tall buildings in a single bound, it's important that you talk with your boss to readjust performance expectations. It's vital that we arrange for meetings to address these issues when they arise, lest the unresolved conflict fester until we blow up like a shaken soda can when the boss asks us to pass the stapler.

Set boundaries. We're responsible for communicating our limits to our employer. If we won't put in a sixty-hour workweek, then it's important that we communicate this. Sticking to our boundaries may hamper advancement, but success at work should *never* be our only gauge of a good life.

Let's do what we can to keep desk rage under control. And to maintain office harmony, let's pay attention to the symptoms of frustration, resolve conflicts constructively, and communicate our boundaries. That'll be good for more than just productivity. It'll be good for the trash cans, too.[52]

THE DISENCHANTED RICH

One of the more popular television shows in recent years has been *Who Wants to Be a Millionaire?* Well, some newly minted millionaires are finding that their new financial success has not translated into happiness. In fact, it's had the opposite effect.

Listen to the words of an anonymous executive when asked about his newfound wealth: "People think, 'You have what everyone dreams of.' What they don't understand is that change is always difficult, and sometimes it's painful. In a lot of ways, I was happier living a simpler life."

The economic boom of the 1990s created thousands just like this executive, newly rich and disillusioned. The problem that's confounding the newly rich has been given a clever name: Sudden Wealth Syndrome. According to clinical psychologist Stephen Goldbart, who coined the term, the new millionaires suffer from isolation, uncertainty, and imbalance.

The bottom line? Luxury cars, expensive vacations, and beautiful homes cannot answer the questions "What is my purpose in life?" and "Who am I?"

When your only purpose in life is to make money, no matter how much you make, there will always be something missing inside. But if your life has greater, more lasting purpose, you will feel fulfilled no matter how poor you are. In a society that has come to worship money, maybe it's time we all stop for a moment and ponder what we should really be living for.

As Goldbart sums it up, "When you ask the wealthy, they will be the first to tell you that wealth doesn't bring you happiness. Part of the problem is that in this country there is no longer a model of what you're supposed to do with your life besides making money."

In the not-so-distant past, it was well accepted that having wealth came with an obligation to reach out to the less fortunate, to help them in their need. Take, for example, Eleanor Roosevelt, who was taught as a child the importance of giving back. She found fulfillment in living her life according to this higher principle. We can, too. I believe that giving to others rather than excessive spending on our own selfish desires will bring us more gratification than possessions ever could.[53]

A MINISTRY IN THE WORKPLACE

hen tragedy struck, killing five members of her family, Cindy Thurman was at a loss about what to do. Devastated by the news that her relatives had died in an automobile accident, Thurman felt completely overwhelmed with the responsibilities involved in arranging for the massive funeral. Her family lacked a close church affiliation, she wasn't familiar with a minister, and she didn't know of a church that could accommodate the large funeral service that would be required for five people.

Fortunately, Thurman's employer, the city of Lufkin, Texas, is one of a growing number of organizations that offers the services of Marketplace Ministries, a company supplying businesses with nonsectarian clergy who provide spiritual, emotional, and practical help to their employees.

Upon learning of Thurman's situation, Marketplace Ministries chaplain Sonny Scarborough sprang into action. He immediately phoned Thurman to offer his condolences and pray with her. Then he quickly located a suitable church and helped the grieving family handle all the details of the funeral.

Scarborough also officiated at the funeral service, which was attended by nearly twelve hundred people. "My only desire," he says, "was to bring hope and meaning in this sudden ending to these earthly lives." Thurman was deeply grateful and asked Scarborough to conduct the upcoming wedding of her daughter.

To date, Marketplace Ministries has assisted with more than fourteen hundred funerals for people who didn't have someone to call on. According to founder Gil Stricklin, one of the best things his ministers do is weep with those who weep.

In addition to helping people like Thurman with funerals—and weddings—Marketplace Ministries chaplains visit hospitalized and homebound employees, offer counseling on marital issues and problems with children, and minister to family members in jails and prisons. Their mission is to be a caring presence in the workplace.

Marketplace Ministries now has 915 chaplains, who serve more than two hundred thousand employees and family members of 240 client companies in thirty-two states. They're making a huge, positive difference, and I highly recommend their work. If you'd like more information about this organization, call them at (800) 775-7657.[54]

SOUND INVESTMENTS

There's a great story about Peter Lynch, the former head of the Fidelity Magellan Fund—perhaps the most popular mutual fund in history. Lynch is about as successful, as affluent a man as you'll find anywhere. He was a Wall Street master, and his colleagues considered him a legend. But at the age of forty-eight he announced a surprising turn in his life. He retired.

Lynch said, "My father died young. I don't want to die at my desk." He was asked what he planned to do. Many thought he'd announce he would become a consultant. Instead, he said he was going to work in his church with kids, declaring, "Kids are a great investment. They beat stocks."

In contrast to Lynch, most of us think of investing in terms of "what do I get out of it?" Some men pursue a relentless quest for investments that will yield the greatest material gain. They end up pouring their best efforts into making a name for themselves in business. Many of us men devote more time and energy to our projects at work than our "projects" at home—our children. But if we will invest in our children's lives, we will see long-lasting yields that money can't buy. If we don't have children living at home, we can invest in the life of another young person—whether it's a fatherless child we know, a grandchild, cousin, nephew, or neighbor.

Great financial investment opportunities will come and go. Meanwhile, the voices of the next generation cry out to us daily. Let's follow the example of Peter Lynch, whose knowledge of life, passion for good, and desire to reach kids took his investing to a whole new level. As the apostle Paul said, "I will very gladly spend for you everything I have and expend myself as well" (2 Corinthians 12:15).

Let's think hard about the things in which we are investing our time and energy. If the balance is tilted toward the superficial or the material, we can decide today to make some changes. This might mean asking our loved ones some touchy questions. We might be in for some painful feedback about how they perceive our priorities. But when we make the necessary adjustments and "invest soundly," the results will pay long-lasting dividends.[55]

Financial Integrity

CREDIT CARD SLAVERY

There's a disease infecting millions of Americans every day. It destroys individuals and families, and it knows no cultural, social, or economic boundaries. The disease? Credit card debt! A study of credit card use by researchers at Ohio State University found that many consumers are involved in a risky financial scheme. They're getting new credit cards to pay off their old ones. What looks like a temporary solution to paying a bill ultimately sends a person spiraling deeper into debt.

Credit card debt is either risk or reality for all American adults. Our culture is constantly encouraging us to "buy, buy, buy" even if we don't have the money. And when our mailboxes are daily billowing with more preapproved credit card offers, it's hard not to get new cards to pay off the old ones.

Those living in debt know that having creditors hanging over their head is like living in slavery. The stress becomes unbearable and causes marital relationships to suffer. Debt damages people's self-esteem, and they begin to wonder whether they'll ever be free of its clutches.

The solution sounds simplistic, but it's the only way to go. We need to pay off our credit cards—and not by getting new ones! One method to prevent overspending is to operate on a cash-only budget. After paying the bills at the beginning of the month, divvy up the remaining cash into envelopes designated for groceries, entertainment, clothing, and so on. When you've emptied an envelope, don't spend any more money that month on that category. This method isn't foolproof because you still have to control your spending, but at least you know exactly how much money you're spending and how much you have left.

Another idea is to stop impulse buying. If you want to buy a nonessential item, try waiting a week before making the purchase. During that week, talk to your spouse or a close friend and ask for advice about the potential purchase. If after a week's time and the consultation you still honestly feel you need the item, and you can afford it, then go and buy it—but not on credit!

We need to be emancipated from credit card slavery so we can experience the joy of financial freedom.

DEATH BY DEBT

The average American household owes several thousand dollars in credit card debt. As the balances rise, they find themselves held hostage financially. Now there is evidence that high amounts of credit card debt can cause physical problems as well. According to Patricia Drentea, professor of sociology at the University of Alabama–Birmingham, people who have more debt seem to suffer more health problems because of the psychological stress that it causes.

Drentea says, "We know there's an association between income and health—we've known that for many years. It's just that since credit cards are a newer kind of economic hardship we weren't sure that it would also show a link. But the stress of debt seems to be associated with higher levels of physical impairments."

Do you lie awake at night worrying about how you'll pay off your credit cards? Do you privately stew every month when you realize you're barely making a dent in your debt because of outrageously high credit card interest rates? Are you doing without necessities because you charged up your credit cards with nonessentials? All of these things would weigh heavily on anyone's shoulders.

In a society that sends the message "You've got to have it now," it's very easy to get caught in debt's deadly snare. Instead of saving money for major purchases, we opt for the "buy now, pay later" plan without a second thought to how we'll pay the debt. As a result, although America has the most robust economy in the world, we also have the lowest savings and highest debt-to-income ratios.

How can you stop the deadly cycle of debt? Well, if you're not in debt, don't let yourself slip into it. Learn to delay personal gratification and resist the temptation to "have it now." If you find yourself mired in debt, draw a line in the sand and say, "No more." Stop spending and start paying things off. You may have to make a lot of sacrifices, but some short-term pain will benefit your long-term financial and physical health.[56]

PAMPERING BABY

A couple of years ago, movie actor Will Smith and his wife, Jada, went shopping for their new baby girl, Willow. Their purchase? An $865 Gucci diaper bag! The Smiths also purchased ten baby baskets stuffed with rhinestone jean jackets for Willow and a $1,280 motorcycle suit for their son, Jaden.

Not to be outdone, rapper Sean "P. Diddy" Combs ordered for his two-year-old son a $5,000 miniature Mercedes-Benz that looks and rides like the real thing. And basketball star Shaquille O'Neal dropped $6,000 for a dollhouse for his daughter.

Obviously, these celebrities have the money to lavish on their children, but more and more middle-class families are also spending exorbitant amounts of money on their children. Parents are "plunking down the plastic" for everything from custom artwork to cars to diamonds and even furs for their little ones.

Sharon Sternheim, owner of an upscale New York department store, says, "Today's generation of parents wants their kids to have the best of everything and are willing to pay for it."

I'm not convinced that more stuff is what our children really need. What they really want is our love and attention. Let's not spend beyond our means to provide them with material goods that will just pass away with time. When they're grown, they're far more likely to look back at their childhood and fondly remember the times we played ball or spent afternoons fishing with them, playing cards with them, or reading to them. They'll remember the stories we told, not the money we spent.

"A good name is more desirable than great riches; to be esteemed is better than silver or gold" (Proverbs 22:1). Our kids will remember the little ways we showed them how much we loved them. Dads, instead of rushing out to spend money on your kids, why not spend time with them? Instead of lavishing them with store-bought presents, give them gifts, like a date with Dad, a family game night, or a family story night. These are the things that will create warm childhood memories that will last a lifetime.[57]

PERSONAL BANKRUPTCY

During 2000 almost 1.5 million individuals in the United States filed for personal bankruptcy. Meanwhile, our nation's banks sent out more than 3.5 billion unsolicited preapproved credit cards. Does anyone see a problem with this?

A recent television ad for a furniture company boasted that it could finance anybody, with no payments for a year. The jingle said, "When you want it, you want it *now!*" What it failed to mention was that while you weren't making payments on your furniture, your 18 percent interest rate was piling up, so when you did start on those payments, you could barely keep your head above water.

The basic tenets of capitalism dictate that the supply of products and services should meet the demand of the consumer market. Fulfilling the American dream of prosperity has always been as theoretically simple as anticipating a consumer need and creating the perfect product to meet that need. This is the American Dream, and it has lured millions of immigrants to our shores in hopes of making it big. However, the goal of the American Dream is not to *meet* needs—it is to create them. The marketers of Sprite, for example, have built a campaign out of the "marketing an image" phenomenon. Their slogan says, "Image is nothing, obey your thirst." At least these guys can make fun of themselves.

The marketers of Sprite know that it doesn't matter to the American people if we are manipulated by advertising. In their eyes, everyone knows it, so they might as well have some fun with it!

But it's not funny anymore.

If we really care about ourselves—and our country—we must reverse this "capitalism gone bad" and take back our wallets, credit cards, and checkbooks. We must realize, despite what our consumer culture dictates, that our fulfillment does not come from buying an image but from realizing that we are created for a purpose by a divine Creator.

TEACH YOUR CHILDREN WELL

Most parents have a hard time talking to their children about sex. It turns out we're avoiding other topics, too. A financial services organization and a social science research firm teamed up to release a survey showing that only 36 percent of parents had taught their children about proper money management. A similar number had talked to them about having good morals and values as well as respecting cultural differences.

Why are so many parents so reluctant to talk with their kids? One expert says, "The theme I consistently get from parents is, 'I know I haven't done well in this myself.' They're afraid of owning up to their shortcomings." But in an era when teenagers are being pressured from all sides with various temptations, it is vitally important that we sit down with them and teach them the life skills to make good choices.

Our society tells them "buy, buy, buy" and "if you don't have the money, there's MasterCard for everything else." Dads, how can our teenagers learn to make wise financial choices without our instruction? The same goes for transmitting solid values to the next generation. Many polls have shown that regardless of what the culture may say, teenagers do greatly value our opinions and teaching. Let's not duck our responsibility! There are simple ways to teach our kids. We've just got to step up.

First, let's sit down with them and have open and frank conversations about the many issues they'll face in life, such as money management, ethics, sexuality, racial tolerance, and so forth. The second step is modeling for them what we've learned from our experiences. If we want our children to handle money properly, we need to show them how to make wise financial decisions and teach them skills such as budgeting and avoiding debt. Let's be open and share our mistakes with our kids so that they can learn from them.

We can take some time with our kids each week and have a one-on-one session on various topics. Let's be vulnerable with them and let them ask us questions. We have a small window of opportunity to influence their lives; let's take advantage of it![58]

TRICKS OF THE TRADE

Picture it. A car lot full of brand-spanking-new minivans. Come to think of it, you *do* need something a little nicer, and it sure would be handy to have all that extra hauling space, more power—and a TV/VCR combo would be great for the next road trip with the kids. A smiling salesman spots you, and it's all over.

Let me relieve a little guilt: It's not all your fault. There are many tricks of the trade that make a shopping trip feel like a grand event. With hot dogs, hamburgers, soft drinks, balloons, tents, and clowns to keep the kids distracted, it's a circus! And the longer you stay, the more likely it is that you'll eventually buy that new vehicle, whether your budget is ready or not.

The primary tool that retailers use is "the happiness factor." In other words, if only you'll buy their stuff, you'll be happy. These experts know us poor shoppers better than we know ourselves. If a sign suggests we buy three, or two for one, or a dozen, more often than not we load up the cart. Really! It's as simple as the power of suggestion.

Here's something else to consider: The next time you're "just looking" at the store, someone else might be "just looking" at you. If you've ever had the bizarre sensation of being watched, maybe somebody was observing your unique buying habits. One New York City firm sends trained observers with video cameras into stores to document shoppers as they're "just looking." Then the store uses that information to determine how to set things out in the store.

How do we survive the games being played? When it comes to a big-ticket item like a minivan, make sure you've got a price in mind before you head to the dealership. Do some research on-line or check the newspaper to comparison shop. Also, if you're buying with a specific purpose in mind, you'll be less likely to purchase on impulse.

Differentiating between needs and wants is tough, but the example of frugal, careful spending is one of the best gifts we can give our children. And no matter how many candy bars the sign tells you to buy, resist the urge![59]

UNSPOILED KIDS

Family budgets can be tight. Even so, we somehow find the cash we need for things that are important. Determining what's important, though, is the tough part—especially when our kids try to "help" us choose our priorities. Kids ask for money almost as often as the car keys. Should we "just say no"?

In 2000, teenagers blew about $84 a week of their own and their parents' money. That's a lot of burgers, fries, CDs, and concert tickets! Just getting the kids dressed for a new school year can cost a mint. A recent survey showed that parents and teens spent on average about $550 for the fashionable look everyone wants.

No matter which tax bracket we're in, if we spend too much money on our kids, we can do them real damage. When we hand them everything on a silver platter—or even in a paper bag—we're robbing them of the sense of struggle and accomplishment that goes along with striving for a goal. How can they appreciate the things money can't buy if their sole focus is acquiring material stuff?

Let's urge our kids to find jobs around the house and neighborhood when they're young. Let them learn responsibility—earn a little extra cash! Be sure to help them open up their own savings account. Most important, train them to wait before spending their money to

SPOILED

avoid the "burning a hole in the pocket" syndrome that even we adults struggle with.

Establishing a budget is also a crucial part of our teaching responsibility. Let's sit down with our children and walk them through a typical month. Without divulging details, let them see that having a place to live costs a lot of money. Help them to see that nothing comes free and very little comes cheap. When they've got enough money to make it worthwhile, help them create their own budget.

Children need to learn that financial independence is a good thing. We must urge them to move out on their own when it comes to money matters. Otherwise, we'll never have the joy of seeing them make solid financial decisions for themselves. We show our respect for their good judgment when we slowly, but surely, force them to stand on their own two feet.[60]

Sports Ethics

ATHLETES AND DOMESTIC VIOLENCE

When pitcher Pedro Astacio, a Dominican national, faced deportation a couple of years ago for beating his wife, the public reaction to his crime was shocking: "Could the Rockies handle this change in their pitching rotation?"

Why is it that domestic violence is often excused when athletes are involved? Even with the increasing frequency of these events, our society often just looks the other way. It seems that we never hear about the women in these situations. The story is always told from the athlete's perspective, as if his wife or girlfriend wasn't really involved in the incident. Often the impact on the team is considered more important than the damage done to the victim.

Some of these athletes are handed out second chances like they're Halloween candy. After all, the team, owners, management, and even the fans have so much invested in these sports stars that they think they can't afford to have them miss any games. The difficulties in an abuser's personal life will just have to be ignored with hopes that they won't affect his performance on game day.

Leniency doesn't help these athletes, and it doesn't honor the suffering of the women involved. Repeated leniency in these matters sends the message to men that domestic violence is okay. But it's not.

And, unfortunately, these crimes happen in millions of homes across America as well, not just with star athletes.

Men, we need to seriously consider the way we deal with anger toward our loved ones. If you've ever abused a girlfriend or a member of your family, you need to take steps to make sure it doesn't happen again. Every man should assess his ability to handle anger—and get the help he needs to bring his anger under control. When you manage your anger with integrity, you become a trusted, safe, and treasured companion to your loved ones. With this goal in mind, I encourage you to practice the self-control necessary for healthy and loving relationships.

161

THE CASE FOR CHARACTER

We've all heard that "character counts," but examples of good character are increasingly hard to come by these days.

A couple of years ago, a professional football player attacked a referee. Was it because of a bad call? No. Did the ref say something inappropriate? No. He threw a flag that *inadvertently* hit the player in the eye. A few seconds later, the player rushed the referee and shoved him to the ground. It was a frightening moment to see this large, imposing man—in full pads, I might add—attack a much smaller person.

I wish I could say it was a rare moment, but not these days. Athletes have methodically gained a license to be violent. A basketball player tried to strangle his coach just a few years ago. He's still playing. Mike Tyson has been welcomed back into boxing even though he tried to bite Evander Holyfield's ear off during a bout.

In sports, spoiled men aren't being held accountable. And if you don't think that affects them later in life, look no further than two of the greatest running backs in pro football history—O. J. Simpson, whose infamous trial needs no further comment; and Jim Brown, who vandalized his wife's car and received a probation sentence. Sadly, the actions of these men are only an extension of what a lot of us would do if given the chance. It's the world we get when no one is called to accountability.

We need to ask ourselves a few questions: Do we do things we know are wrong because we believe we can get away with them? Do we mistreat someone who we know can't do anything about it? Do we lie to our spouse—just on the little things that we think won't matter? Is a crude joke more important to us than the people we offend? These are common character flaws that truly shape who we are—and controlling them is one way to affect our own character.

Men, if you need help to control these flaws, I encourage you to seek out a small group of close friends who will hold you accountable in the area of character. We all need accountability because character *does* count.

A FATHER, A SON, AND A FASTBALL

Would you quit your job if your boss wouldn't let you bring your teenage son to work with you? In a move that made both history and headlines, Oakland A's pitcher Doug Jones included an unusual clause in his player's contract—his oldest son, fifteen-year-old Dustin.

In his forties and tired of spending most of the baseball season away from his family, Doug decided to get creative with his signing options and demonstrate his commitment to his son. He made it clear that he wouldn't sign a new contract unless the team worked it out to keep his kids involved.

So Dustin worked in the A's clubhouse, traveled with the team on road trips, hustled the team's gear, and spent valuable time bonding with his father as his roommate on the road. Dustin got a real-life education about a career that many only dream about. Doug got something more: irreplaceable, hands-on time in the life of his teenage son.

You may not be able to negotiate your working environment like a big league baseball player, but where's your "line in the sand"? What are you willing to give up for more time with your family?

Doug Jones took a good look at what was precious and put his $650,000 contract on the line. The Oakland A's worked it out because Doug was critical to their bullpen. The outcome wasn't guaran-

NSTRATE

teed, but to Doug it was worth the risk. What are you willing to risk for the things that are precious in your life?

The next time you're inclined to work late, remember this creed: Fifty years from now no one will remember what kind of car you drove, what kind of house you lived in, what social groups you belonged to, or how much money was in your bank account. But the world will be different because of what you did or did not do in the lives of your children.

We don't have to be professional athletes in order to take a stand for our convictions. All we need is a sense of who we are as fathers, husbands, and men. We can choose to live out our priorities like they're the most important things in our life—because they are.[61]

SPORTS ETHICS

IS HONESTY ALWAYS
THE BEST POLICY?

Jan Gangelhoff made a significant contribution to the men's basketball program at the University of Minnesota. She helped players stay eligible by writing, or assisting in writing, hundreds of papers and assignments between 1994 and 1998.

The cheating started innocently enough. Gangelhoff was an executive secretary in the athletic department and tutored players. Over time she started to assist in writing their papers. Eventually, to save time, she was writing some of the papers herself. She knew that her cheating was wrong, and eventually she confessed to save her peace of mind. Her confession brought down the basketball program.

Gangelhoff paid a high price for her cheating and confession. She lost her job and many friendships, her health declined from stress, and her once black hair became salt-and-pepper gray. Also, she lost touch with the players who once considered her a combination tutor and den mother. The scandal caused so much suffering that Gangelhoff said she wonders if she should have confessed. She survived, but the cost was high.

Sometimes it's tempting to cheat or lie about little things. That's probably what Gangelhoff thought when she wrote that first paper. But wrong behavior that starts small can easily snowball out of control. And the price paid for wrongdoing often escalates right along with it. Whether it's an academic scandal, unethical business dealings, cheating on taxes, or lying to friends—it's hard to change our behavior once we've started doing something wrong. That's why it's vital to practice ethical living from the beginning. The University of Minnesota scandal would have been much easier to avert if someone had taken a stand when the cheating began.

Men, let's practice ethical behavior in everything we do. Perhaps your company overbills clients, or maybe there's something your wife needs to know but you haven't told her. I encourage you to come clean and practice right behavior. In the long run, doing the right thing saves a lot of pain. The cost of honesty may seem high, but the payoff is huge! Clean living brings peace of mind and less stress because we no longer have anything to hide.[62]

SHAME OF THE GAMES

At the 1936 Olympic Games in Berlin, German dictator Adolf Hitler hoped to prove the Nazi myth of Aryan superiority. Unfortunately for Hitler, American heroes Jesse Owens, Ralph Metcalfe, Foy Draper, and Frank Wycoff, two of them black, easily won gold for the United States in the 400-meter relay.

Although the American team's victory was a triumph, the tragedy of the 400-meter relay race was that two Jewish runners should have been competing for the U.S. team. Marty Glickman and Sam Stoller were on the team until race day, when without explanation, they were told they wouldn't be running.

Glickman and Stoller returned home as the only U.S. Olympians not to compete in Berlin. The exact details of the race remain a mystery. Of course, it's not documented that anti-Semitism kept the men from running, but the two men—and even Metcalfe, who did run in the race—agreed that the Jews were held out for political reasons. Certain powerful people didn't want to see Hitler "shown up" by Jewish athletes.

Sadly, a gold medal marking one of our country's defining moments became an illustration of racism. An otherwise glorious achievement was darkened by injustice. Those who haven't experienced racism firsthand might be tempted to say it no longer exists.

But racism was a cancer in 1936, and it continues to hurt the progress of our country today. Racism creates questions and insecurity, and it allows evil to roam free in its darkness.

Men, let's work to overcome racism and its effects. First, we can expose it, and then we can refuse to tolerate it. When we see racism or prejudice around us, let's take a stand against it and let the world know that it's not acceptable to treat someone unequally because of race or ethnic heritage.

Let's work toward a day when, as the great Martin Luther King Jr. said, "A man is judged not by the color of his skin, but by the content of his character." And, men, may the content of our character uphold the value of the human race.[63]

WHEELCHAIR COACH
"KICKS IT" IN THE NFL

He's never played a down of football, but he's the kicking coach for the Miami Dolphins. Like so many boys, Doug Blevins dreamed of being a football hero, but cerebral palsy denied this dream. Stuck in a wheelchair, but with ferocious determination, Blevins set his sights on a different dream.

"I knew I'd never play a down," Blevins says. "But I was set on this goal: making it to the National Football League. I knew that whatever I did, . . . I had to be the best in the country."

He reviewed football guides. He filled notebooks during televised games. He attended coaching camps and obsessively reviewed replays. And, after spending a lifetime studying the game, Blevins is now one of the world's foremost authorities on kicking a football.

At home he'd go with his cousins to the field and instruct them in leg swings, hip swivels, and other movements his body couldn't perform. While other guys practiced, he sat with the coaches, picking their brains.

After earning a football coaching scholarship from the University of Tennessee, Blevins formed his own consulting company. He named it Championship Placekicking and Punting. His reputation grew quickly. In a game that often comes down to special teams, he became an asset. Before long, NFL teams were calling for his expertise. Finally, the Dolphins hired him as their kicking coach.

Blevins says that he has "a little cerebral palsy" and refuses to use a disability sticker in his car. He operates under this simple life philosophy: "If you stop accomplishing, you stagnate."

I think it's time we apply Blevins's philosophy to our relationships. "Accomplishing" means that we initiate reconciliation when we've hurt our wife. Accomplishing means that we don't let bad blood fester between us and a coworker. It means that we learn to humble ourselves in order to save relationships. Accomplishing means that we don't allow ourselves to slack off when it comes to serving others. If we stop accomplishing, we will stagnate—and so will our relationships.

Doug Blevins has done what many thought impossible. If we're willing to challenge ourselves in our relationships, we too are capable of amazing things.[64]

WORLD-CLASS HUMILITY

Kip Keino, an uncoached Nandi tribesman from Kenya, burst onto the world track and field scene at the 1968 Summer Olympics in Mexico City. There, he had a legendary showdown with Jim Ryun of the United States.

Ryun was a heavy favorite in the race. In fact, he hadn't been beaten in the 1500 meters in more than three years. Then, on the day of the race, Keino got caught in traffic on the way and was forced to jog the last mile to the stadium. Still, against all odds, Keino won the race by an astounding 20 meters.

Four years later at the Munich Games, Keino added another chapter to his legacy. After placing second in the 1500 meters, he entered the 3000-meter steeplechase as a challenge. He won the gold medal, setting an Olympic record.

Keino's Olympic glory made him one of the most recognizable faces in sub-Saharan Africa. However, despite his fame, he always remained humble and used his fortune to help others. Although famous enough to ride in limousines, he chose instead to drive an old four-door Nissan with a busted speedometer and no hubcaps. In a world dominated by me-first athletes, Keino and his wife, Phyllis, have shown that grace, selflessness, and heartfelt devotion to others can accomplish great things.

Over the years the Keinos have taken in more than one hundred orphaned and abandoned children and given them hope and love. Keino says, "I came into this world with nothing. I will leave with nothing. While I am here, I should be mindful of those people who need help. They need food. They need clothing. They need shelter. They need love."

I don't know about you, but it's hard for me to be humble. I want a nice car and a nice house. I want a comfortable life. I'm challenged by the story of Kip and Phyllis Keino and the sacrifices they've made for others. Am I living for myself, or am I living for others? When we commit to a life of humility, we'll have the resources to help others and make a difference in their lives.[65]

Race Relations

AN UNBROKEN PROMISE

When Navajo pastor John Tso moved to take a pastorate on the southern edge of the Navajo nation, he knew it meant living in an old trailer. After a number of years, Pastor Tso was hoping to find a way to build a house. That's when he attended one of the Promise Keepers mass gatherings of men, Stand in the Gap, on October 7, 1997, in Washington, D.C.

There, Pastor Tso met George Tellez, an Anglo-Hispanic man from Dallas, who owned a construction company. In a brief conversation, Tellez learned of Tso's living circumstances and quickly promised to build the Navajo pastor a house—for free!

A nice gesture, thought Tso, as they exchanged phone numbers. But he didn't believe for a moment that he'd ever hear from the man again. After all, white men had been making and breaking promises to Native Americans for centuries. But soon after he returned home, he received a call from Tellez.

To make a long story short, Tellez proved to be a man of his word. Yes, it took a while, and there were delays in the process. During an eight-month period when the two men didn't see each other, Pastor Tso was assailed by nagging doubts, even though the two men stayed in touch.

He means well, Tso thought, *but Mr. Tellez is a very busy man.* His

skepticism soon gave way, however, as a house began to take shape—something Pastor Tso often refers to as "the awesome thing that was happening before my eyes." Completed a month before the one-year anniversary of their meeting, a three-bedroom, two-bathroom home now sits on the spot formerly occupied by the old house trailer.

Asked what had prompted him to take on such a project, Tellez replied, "In the past, Native Americans were promised a lot. I just wanted to give something back." Men, we too can reach out to those different from ourselves. In so doing, George Tellez helped to break down barriers of distrust. Since then, the two men have gotten to know each other better and have developed a mutual respect. They've become friends. And there is power in that friendship.[66]

MEDIA CONTRIBUTE TO
RACIAL MISUNDERSTANDING

Do blacks and Hispanics commit more crime? Some people think so.

When Matt was honest, he admitted that he thought twice whenever he passed a group of black guys hanging out on a street corner. He also let on that he locked his car doors whenever he drove through "the hood." Matt doesn't feel good about his prejudice. But like many other whites, he has the perception that he's more likely to be victimized by a minority than by a Caucasian. Recent research supports the contrary. In reality, a white person is actually three times more likely to be victimized by another white person than by a minority.

This misperception is common. And who's to blame? In part, it's a result of the media's presentation of minority crime. "The best research indicates that crime coverage doesn't reflect crime trends," reports the *Los Angeles Times*. Experts say that the news media, particularly TV news, unduly connect race with violent crime. In the news, minorities are overrepresented when compared with the actual proportion of crimes they commit.

One way to solve this problem is for all of us to keep the media in perspective—to realize that the news outlets profit by presenting sensational information. They often go to extremes to attract attention.

We shouldn't blindly accept what we hear from the media or any other source. All of our perspectives should be well informed by facts and by personal research and experience.

Men, it's time for a nationwide dialogue between races. Let's try asking our friends and acquaintances of different racial backgrounds what they think of the media's portrayal of race. Their answers will educate us and, I hope, give us a better understanding of these issues.

Getting to know people from other races will personalize the issues. We'll no longer naïvely watch TV reports and think that we need to fear people of other races. We'll be able to keep the news reports in perspective and give them only the credibility they deserve. If we commit to an interracial dialogue, maybe we can eliminate some of the ignorance that allows racial prejudice to divide our country.

A QUESTION OF COLOR

A friendly three-year-old African-American girl walked up to a middle-aged white man in a shopping mall and said, "Hi! Give me a hug." According to the girl's mother, the man looked at her like he was going to vomit.

In an instant, children can be thrust into the hateful world of bigotry, suddenly being made aware that the color of their skin matters. Many would like to believe that prejudice is a problem of the past—but present events tell us otherwise. A well-known Internet service provider is hosting hate clubs. Homes and places of worship are still being vandalized and burned. Racially motivated attacks and beatings occur daily.

It doesn't escape a child's notice that all U. S. presidents have been white men. Our children hear the racially stereotyped jokes. If we, as fathers, don't address this problem, our children will grow up thinking that these attitudes are acceptable. We must teach our children that prejudice and discrimination are wrong. How do we stop this curse from being passed to yet another generation?

We can start by accepting our children as unique and special. According to research by the Anti-Defamation League, children who feel good about themselves are less likely to be prejudiced. We can help our children to be sensitive to others' feelings. We can step out of our comfort zones and establish relationships with families of ethnic groups other than our own.

Men, we must take the lead by taking appropriate action against prejudice and discrimination. When others use bigoted language around us and our children, let's show by our actions and our words that it's unacceptable. Often, it's as simple as saying, "That kind of joke offends me," or "Please don't talk that way around my family."

What do we do if our children experience the hatred of prejudice like the little girl I mentioned? From a child's point of view, race relations are about feelings, self-esteem, respect, and simplicity. In the end, young children who've encountered prejudice mainly want to be comforted. The girl's mother, Sherry Davis Molock, director of the clinical psychology program at Howard University, suggests we keep it simple. Tell your child, "If someone thinks you're yucky, it's their problem. There's nothing wrong with you."[67]

RACISM AT PENN STATE

Here's a quote to think about: "This is a white academy in a white town in a white county—and by God it's going to stay that way. We are determined to rid this place of the black blight on our community. Those like you have been run off or killed. You will also disappear."

Is this some hate-filled letter left over from the 1950s or 1960s when race relations between blacks and whites in our country were appalling? No. Sadly enough, it's a letter received on April 20, 2001, by LaKeisha Wolf, president of the Black Caucus at Penn State University.

Yes, racial hatred has once again reared its ugly head on an American university campus, and the hatred's not restricted to a few barbaric students. According to *Newsweek* magazine, Penn State has been a place where black students have felt unwelcome, isolated, and uncomfortable for a long time. Wolf now feels compelled to wear a bulletproof vest and is escorted by bodyguards provided by the university.

Many of us in the white community feel as if the race problem has been solved. And although it's true that much progress has been made, we have a long way to go when some of the best and brightest of our white students in one of our top universities can make life terrifying for some of the best and brightest black students.

The sad and sorry history of race relations in this great country has wounds too fresh and bloody for any university to stand by and watch. Student protesters were able to jolt the university into making some minor changes, but a respected institution of higher education has to do more than that. If there's anything our college students need to learn in our universities, it's that racial hatred is one of the most evil and destructive forces born from the bowels of hell itself. There's no place for people to hate one another on the basis of skin color—or for any other reason.[68]

THE STATE OF THE BLACK FAMILY

According to the United States Census Bureau, black Americans are the most "unpartnered" segment of our society. Some observers believe that the future of black marriages is in doubt. This generation of young black adults has seen firsthand the struggles of many black marriages and families, and has been profoundly affected by it. The statistics are staggering: Forty-seven percent of the country's 8.4 million black households are led by single mothers. Fifty-four percent of black Americans between the ages of twenty-four and thirty-four have never married.

Black husbands, in particular, struggle. Often they are perceived by our society as angry and dangerous. As a result, they often have problems with intimacy. Eric Wayne Powell, a social worker and minister who has a successful marriage, says that although sharing intimate thoughts does not come easily to men as a whole, that "goes double for black men. They have not been socialized to share [their] pain and frustration."

Nevertheless, there is hope for the black family. Despite the gloomy statistics and forecasts, there *are* black couples who are making it. What is the secret to their success? A strong spiritual base. The Powells, for example, attribute their success to having strong moral principles and faith in God. Powell says, "We definitely know that without that, any marriage would be extremely difficult."

In addition, those who have a strong faith are less likely to engage in premarital sex or have a child out of wedlock, all predicators of future marital and economic failure. "The young African-American man or woman who was raised in the church is apt to do the right thing, eventually," Powell says. "They see marriage as necessary to maintain morality and values."

What is true for the black family is true for all families. A strong spiritual base is integral to the family's success. All of us, regardless of our race, need to reject the stereotype of black men that has been portrayed in our society and celebrate the men who lead successful black families. Finally, we need to support the black churches, which provide a spiritual anchor for families.[69]

TULSA RACE RIOTS

It may have been the largest occasion of racial violence in U.S. history. Beginning May 31, 1921, two hundred to three hundred innocent blacks died in two days of fighting in Tulsa, Oklahoma. The riot broke out when a white lynch mob clashed with blacks, who were protecting a black man accused of assaulting a white woman. Over the next two days, white mobs set fire to homes, businesses, and churches in Greenwood, a thriving black business district, known then as the Black Wall Street of America.

There were reports of airplanes bombing blacks and of bodies being thrown into the Arkansas River. There were also stories of mass graves—men, women, and children tossed anonymously into the ground.

When it was over, many people left Tulsa and never returned. The National Guard rounded up thousands of blacks and imprisoned them at the fairgrounds, convention hall, and a baseball stadium.

Justice was never done. It was a massacre lost in the pages of history, virtually unreported by white historians—until now. A state of Oklahoma commission, after two years of study, has recommended that reparations be paid, at long last, to the victims of the riot. The proposed restitution will take the form of college scholarships, direct payments to survivors and descendants, and a program to help fund economic development in Greenwood, along with a memorial to the dead.

Is it right to worry about something that happened so long ago? After all, most of us had nothing to do with the riots—and most of those who did are long gone. But time doesn't run out on injustice in a fair and just country. Many innocent blacks were killed in the riots, and most of a prosperous and thriving black community was destroyed, never to be seen again in its former state.

If we demand that justice be done for the victims of the Holocaust or for the victims of ethnic cleansing in Kosovo or Rwanda, then no less should be expected for our fellow citizens. We can't pretend that Tulsa's race riots didn't happen or that justice was realized for its victims and survivors. It was not. Fear, distrust, and damage are the echoes that call out for a response. Trying to make it right is the only right thing to do.

Culture & Common Sense

ARE YOU ALITERATE?

Are you aliterate? I don't mean illiterate, but *a*literate. Unlike illiterate folks, aliterate people know how to read; however, they choose to get their information by watching television or videos, or listening to things like audio books, rather than through written material. According to social commentator Chuck Colson, this practice is becoming a trend in America—a trend that isn't necessarily good.

Have you noticed that grocery stores, fast-food restaurants, and children's videos are all replacing words with colors, shapes, and icons? This trend appears to be part of the "dumbing down" of our society. Colson reports that ten years ago most Americans read at least thirty minutes a day but now only 45 percent of us do. And even though more people are reading on the Internet, they're usually scanning for information, not engaging in real thought. The trouble is, says TV critic Neil Postman, acquiring information from television and the Web encourages a short attention span, disjointed thinking, and purely emotional responses. And I would add *passivity* to the list.

Is it any wonder that people are so easily influenced by fast-paced media and advertising campaigns, image over substance, and emotional appeals over well-thought-out arguments? Colson goes so far as to state that the new visual media created by modern technology may actually be undermining literacy. After all, only so much can be learned from pictures and images, right?

By way of contrast, the value of reading goes beyond obtaining information. It demands thoughtful analysis, sustained attention, and an active imagination. So what about you? Have you read a good book lately? Perhaps more important, are you encouraging your children to read and to develop a love for reading?

Men, let's set an example for our families by being readers ourselves. Instead of passively sitting in front of the boob tube or even the PC for hours on end, let's actively feed our mind by reading. Let's also make a point of discussing ideas and issues at the dinner table. By doing these things, maybe we can smarten up and help turn the tide against the dumbing down of America.[70]

AUTOBIOGRAPHY OF AN ALCOHOLIC

The abuse of alcohol can tear a man apart. I know this firsthand. My date was in tears. She and her girlfriend were terrified that I was going to kill us all on the icy road. I wasn't too concerned. I was drunk. Angry. I gunned the gas, swerving my borrowed car through the snowbound lanes of Columbia, Missouri.

Crunch! We slammed into a parked police car.

It was winter 1961. I was a lineman on the University of Missouri football team, and I had a huge problem with alcohol. My date happened to be Lyndi, my future wife, and you could say that our relationship was off to a shaky start. Unfortunately for me, the policeman was in his car at the time I rammed into it. He approached my window, leaned in, and asked me to get out of the car. I replied, "I don't think you're big enough to get me out of this car!" He didn't need to. Lyndi shoved me out herself, and before I knew it I was in handcuffs.

My debacle with the policeman resulted in the loss of my football scholarship. I was devastated. Football was my life, and I'd been disgraced. My alcoholism overcame me, and my willpower was useless against it. Fortunately, because of that acknowledgment, combined with faith and time, I've been given my life back.

Sadly, struggles like mine are common. The National Institute on Alcohol Abuse and Alcoholism reports that nearly fourteen million

Americans abuse alcohol or are alcoholics. *Five Deadly Vices,* a book by Raul Ries, blames alcohol for the deaths of more than one hundred thousand Americans annually. We've got to attack this problem head on!

The NIAAA has some suggestions for overcoming alcohol abuse. First, recognize the problem. If you wonder whether you have a problem, ask those closest to you what they think. After recognizing the problem, get help! Treatment may include individual, marriage, or family counseling, and attending Alcoholics Anonymous meetings.

Men, let's regain control of our life by winning the battle against alcohol. Thanks to the grace of God, I'm winning that battle now, and my life is all the better for it.[71]

THE COST OF CELL PHONES

The name of the game today is multitasking. We're trying to squeeze more into a day, even making our commute productive. But any kind of multitasking behind the wheel can be dangerous. Whether we're flipping channels on the radio, fishing for something under the seat, or snatching a glance at the sports section, we're putting others at risk because of fleeting momentary concerns. Just ask Niki Taylor.

In the fashion industry, there are models, and then there are supermodels. It takes grace, talent, beauty, plus that little something extra to make it to supermodel status. Niki Taylor fits the bill, but on April 29, 2001, she almost died when a man who was driving her home took his eyes off the road to pick up his cell phone. In that brief moment, he lost control of the car, which jumped the curb and smashed into a utility pole. Taylor was rushed to the hospital, suffering from a torn liver and other internal injuries. The driver of the car later commented that nothing on the phone "can be nearly as important as what's going on in front of you."

This near fatal accident, with its terrible lingering consequences, brought attention to a big problem: dialing while driving. There's a bumper sticker out there that says it all: "Drive now, talk later." That simple message should be taken to heart. Police, state legislators, and local activists are fed up and agree that something must be done. A few cities and counties have passed laws restricting cell phone use while driving. More will no doubt follow. Automobile insurers are considering a surcharge on premiums for drivers who use cell phones.

Here's a startling statistic: One study found that collision rates for drivers using handheld cell phones were roughly the same as for drivers who were legally drunk. Apparently, distracted drivers are unsafe at any speed! Keeping our eyes on the road should be at the top of every "to do" list. It's simple. When you want to use the car phone, pull over safely to the side of the road. It could save lives.[72]

MANNERS AND CIVILITY

The tone of the rhetoric in Washington, D.C., has been decidedly bitter in recent years, reaching new lows in the 2000 presidential election. Thankfully, that seems to have changed for the better since President Bush took office—and the tragic events of September 11, 2001—and I hope it bodes well for our country.

Unfortunately, civility and manners seem to be increasingly rare in our society today. Professional athletes use profanity on camera and boast about moves that injure opposing players. On the field, some players shamelessly taunt the other team every time they make a play. It seems like rudeness and vulgarity are the order of the day. The prevalence of road rage on our highways, people using cell phones in theaters and restaurants, and the disrespect many young people show for authority are also indicators of a general decline of manners in our society.

Sue Fox, author of the book *Etiquette for Dummies,* says, "We seem to have become a society that is self-absorbed, self-consumed, self-centered, and [self-]righteous. All of this can be considered rude behavior."

Dads, whatever the state of our society, it's our job to teach our kids to exercise good manners, behave civilly, and respect authority. Much of that involves how we teach them to interact with us, their siblings, and others. It starts with simple things, like teaching our kids to say please and thank you, to address adults as Mr. and Mrs., and to respect the property of others by requesting permission before using something.

Not only must we demand respect from our kids, we must expect them to show respect for all adults, including teachers, policemen, and others in authority.

When it comes to sports, our children need to hear from us that "flaunting and taunting" show poor sportsmanship and should be discouraged. Of course, if they see that we enjoy those kinds of displays when watching athletic events, our words will have no effect.

I hope that the new tone of civility in our nation's capital will take hold and then filter down to our sports fields, schoolyards, and homes. It's high time for a return to manners and civility all across America.[73]

PRODUCTIVE LIVES

Have you ever wanted to go back to school? Ever thought you'd try your hand at gardening? Remember all the goals you dreamed up as a kid? That was before your life got busy and more complicated, right?

Sometimes it's easy to become comfortable with the status quo. We leave goal setting for New Year's Day. We leave book writing and marathon running to others. We neglect the ideals that once inspired us. It's as if our dreams expired with our youth. We become stagnant. Worse yet, we're virtually unaffected by our own standstill.

Did you know that Pablo Picasso continued to produce drawings when he was ninety years old? His paintings became more innovative each year. Pianist Arthur Rubinstein gave one of his greatest performances at eighty-nine. And the actress Jessica Tandy? She won an Academy Award at eighty.

These people continued to lead productive lives in spite of their age and the restraints that society would place on them. I'm inspired by these lives. They're stories of those who pressed on. They realized their work was not yet finished. Neither is ours.

Life is too precious to be spent at an impasse. Let's not let another day pass us by without considering our purpose. Let's set realistic goals for ourselves and for our relationships—and then outline strategies for their achievement.

Is it your goal to do more to nurture your marriage? Is there a book you've always wanted to read—or write? Is there a language you've considered learning? Maybe you'll strive to develop a neglected part of your character. Or maybe you'll sit down with your family to write a family mission statement that brings focus and unity to your home. Whatever it is, men, let's challenge ourselves to live life the way it was meant to be lived: in continual pursuit of growth.

What contributions do you always wish you had made? Don't abandon those dreams! Maybe it's time to bring those ideas to life. After all, a goal is nothing more than a dream with a deadline and a written plan of action. Remember, as the actor John Barrymore is reputed to have said, "A man is not yet old till regrets take the place of dreams."[74]

SLEEPWALKERS

Hey! Are you yawning again? I'm tired, too. Maybe it's time to call a halt to sleep deprivation!

Babies get all the breaks. They're carried, coddled, and cared for—and, best of all, they get regular nap times. Required sleep—that's the life for me! Unfortunately, most of us don't have it quite so good. A poll by the National Sleep Foundation showed that at least 63 percent of Americans aren't getting the nightly eight hours of sleep they need. In fact, we're putting in more hours at work and getting less snooze time than we did five years ago.

Have you ever fallen asleep during your favorite movie? Or, worse yet, during a good-night kiss from your wife? Things have got to change! Sleep deprivation is becoming a critical problem. Thinking slows down with lack of sleep, and reaction time is clearly affected when we haven't done some serious dozing. Don't we all want the fast driver in the next lane to have had plenty of sleep?

When we're up too late or working too hard, our brains have trouble concentrating. Without enough sleep, memory becomes weak and creativity suffers. Even though we think we're doing our best at work, performance can suffer without appropriate rest at night. In others words, we can put in fewer hours on the job and work at higher efficiency if we'll only get enough sleep.

Solving this problem can be tough. Slashing hours at work may be difficult, but when we stop seeing ourselves as indispensable, maybe our eyes will open to some practical ways to cut out the extra hours. For example, regular exercise will help relax both the mind and body. Perhaps the simplest solution is to set a regular schedule and get to bed on time. The room should be quiet and free from distractions like phones and the TV. Another trick is to turn the clock around to face the wall so you don't anxiously watch the hours tick away. Never eat or drink within three hours of retiring. And, whatever you do, don't spend the night worrying about tomorrow.

Let's give ourselves a break and get to bed early tonight.[75]

TECHNOLOGY'S EFFECT
ON RELATIONSHIPS

A friend related this scene to me. A man and woman sat in a coffee shop, apparently on a date. The guy's cell phone kept ringing—and it must have been important business because he made his attractive companion wait as he took the calls. For about fifteen minutes he was on and off his phone numerous times. Finally, when yet another call came in, his date produced her own cell phone and started making some calls of her own. Some date!

Technology has definitely changed human interaction. In fact, we don't really need to talk to people face-to-face anymore. We can use cell phones, voice mail, and e-mail to talk to each other. Our meetings no longer require that we even be in the same country. Now we can have our groceries delivered to our home and do all our shopping on the Internet. If we wanted to, it seems we could totally remove people from our life!

Technology does make life more efficient, but when we make efficiency our top priority, we can subconsciously start viewing human interaction as inconvenient, unproductive, and unnecessary. This creates an internal struggle because we've been created to be in relationship with other people. When we simply coexist as independent entities in a computer-run culture, we become lonely and unfulfilled. It is vital to all of us that we know and are known by other people. Let's not merely transmit data back and forth to each other.

I'm not against technology, but we've got to make conscious decisions about how it will influence our relationships. We must recognize the ways in which technological advances impede our ability to relate interpersonally. Let's set some boundaries to protect our most important relationships. Let's challenge ourselves to speak directly to friends, even though we could leave them a voice mail or send an e-mail. Also, let's not be controlled by our phones! Let's turn off our cell phones in the evenings. When we're with family, let's really be with family 100 percent. We've got to be deliberate about making *people* a priority. When we do this, our relationships will stay strong in this technological age.

Notes

1. Information for this article adapted from Joe White, *What Kids Wish Parents Knew about Parenting* (West Monroe, La.: Howard Publishing Co., Inc., 1998), as quoted on <www.crosswalk.com>, "How to Live Happily through the Teenage Years: You Don't Need a Barrel," 11 April 2001.

2. Information for this article adapted from Gary Smalley and John Trent, *The Hidden Value of a Man* (Colorado Springs: Focus on the Family Publishing, 1994), and James Dobson, *Straight Talk* (Dallas: Word Publishing, 1995).

3. Information for this article adapted from Bill Becher, "Bike Father, Bike Son," *Los Angeles Daily News,* 14 June 2001.

4. Information for this article adapted from Roberto Rivera, "What Do Boys Need?" *Citizen,* March 2000, 28–29.

5. Information for this article adapted from Carl Auerbach and Louise Silverstein, "Deconstructing the Essential Father," *American Psychologist* (June 1999); and "Less Child Neglect When Dad Is Involved in Upbringing," Reuters, 16 February 2000; <www.reuters.com>.

6. Information for this article adapted from a story in the *Chattanooga Times/Chattanooga Free Press,* 3 February 2001, sec. 3A.

7. Information for this article adapted from David Popenoe, "Single Father's Day," *The Weekly Standard,* 2 July 2001; see also <marriage.rutgers.edu>.

8. Information for this article adapted from "Too Many Parents Aren't Making the Grade," *Rocky Mountain News,* 11 November 2000.

9. Information for this article adapted from Edward J. Boyer, "Getting Children Hooked on Golf," *Los Angeles Times,* 31 March 2001.

10. Information for this article adapted from Tamar Lewin, "Survey Shows Sex Practices of Boys," *New York Times,* 19 December 2000.

11. Information for this article adapted from "Just Say No," *Rocky Mountain News,* 21 January 2001.

12. Information for this article adapted from "Study: Peers Sway a Child's Interest in Smoking, Drinking as Early as Sixth Grade," CNN, 23 January 2001; and "Teen Drinking a Sign of Problems to Come," Reuters, 23 January 2001; <www.reuters.com>.

13. Information for this article adapted from "Children from Intact Families More Likely to Abstain from Sex," Family Research Council, *Culturefacts,* 7 February 2001.

14. Information for this article adapted from Katy Kelly, "Get That TV Out of Your Children's Bedroom," *U. S. News & World Report,* 29 November 1999.

15. Information for this article adapted from "Students Hear Call for Safer Drug Use," *Rocky Mountain News,* 10 April 2001.

16. Information for this article adapted from "But Scientists Link Tattoos to Crime," 30 April 2001; <www.thetimes.co.uk>.

17. Information for this article adapted from "If Mom OKs Birth Control, Teen Sex More Likely," Reuters, 31 August 2000; <www.reuters.com>; The National Campaign to Prevent Teen Pregnancy; and "Parent Chats Pass Sex Attitudes to Teens," *USA Today,* 7 March 2000.

18. Information for this article adapted from "The Value of Commitment," 10 January 2001; <www.crosswalk.com>.

19. Information for this article adapted from "Are You Headed for Divorce? First Two Years Can Tell," Reuters, 22 February 2001; <www.reuters.com>.

20. Information for this article adapted from Steven K. Paulson, "Divorce Prevention Said Flawed," Associated Press, 30 June 2000; <www.ap.org>; and Karen S. Peterson, "The Marriage Manifesto," *USA Today,* 29 June 2000.

21. Information for this article adapted from Karen S. Peterson, "Taking Inventory of Happy Couples," *USA Today,* 7 February 2000.

22. Information for this article adapted from "A Fine Romance for Zeta and Michael," *Daily Express;* and "All Eyes on Catherine and Michael"; <itn.co.uk>.

23. Information for this article adapted from Karen S. Peterson, "Late Night Shift Takes Toll on Marriages," *USA Today,* 2 February 2000.

24. Information for this article adapted from "Love Can Lower Blood Pressure," *Rocky Mountain News,* 22 May 2001.

25. Information for this article adapted from <www.newswise.com>.

26. Information for this article adapted from *Youth Today,* September 2000.

27. Information for this article adapted from "A Prelude to Divorce," *New Man,* July/August 2000; and Kerby Anderson, "Living Together," 8 October 1998; <www.probe.org>.

28. Information for this article adapted from "Couch Potato Mitch Hallen Loves Watching His Television So Much That He's Married It," MegaStar News, 14 January 2001; <www.megastar.co.uk>.

29. Information for this article adapted from Timothy Dailey, "Singles Seeking Self-Fulfillment or Soul Mate?" *Washington Watch,* July 2001; and Christine Hall, "Married, Biological Parents Best for Child, Research Shows," 24 July 2001; <www.crosswalk.com>.

30. Information for this article adapted from Kathleen Kelleher, "So There Are More Single People, But It's Still a Couples' World," *Los Angeles Times,* 12 February 2001.

31. Information for this article adapted from "It Takes a Town," ABC News, 28 March 2001.

32. Information for this article adapted from "Aggressive Driving Poses Safety Threat," *Amica Today,* summer 2001; and "But Officer . . . ," *U. S. News & World Report,* 26 March 2001.

33. Information for this article adapted from <www.abc.net.au/worldtoday>; and <www.news.bbc.co.uk>.

34. Information for this article adapted from Marshall Allen, "He Chose Death," *Echo*, spring 1999.

35. Information for this article adapted from an article in the *Colorado Springs Gazette*, 11 May 2001.

36. David B. Wardell and Jeffrey A. Leever, *Daily Disciples* (Uhrichsville, Ohio: Promise Press, 2001), 161.

37. Information for this article adapted from Jennifer Ragland, "A Jewel of a Janitor," *Los Angeles Times*, 28 April 2001.

38. Information for this article adapted from Don Jacobs, "Ticket to Read," *Knoxville News-Sentinel*, reprinted in *Reader's Digest*, March 2001.

39. Information for this article adapted from John Markoff, "Portrait of a Newer, Lonelier Crowd Is Captured in Internet Survey," *New York Times*, 16 February 2000; and Merritt McKinney, "Compulsive Computer Use Is Growing," Reuters, 7 February 2000; <www.reuters.com>.

40. Fred Stoeker and Stephen Arterburn, *Every Man's Battle: Winning the War on Sexual Temptation One Victory at a Time* (Colorado Springs: WaterBrook Press, 2000).

41. Information for this article adapted from Ashley Dunn, "Hooked on Games Online," *Los Angeles Times*, 12 May 2000.

42. Information for this article adapted from Kate N. Grossman, "'Hefner Way' Stirs Chicago Debate," Associated Press, 11 April 2000; <www.ap.org>; and "Bob Crane," *Biography*, A&E Network, 2000.

43. Information for this article adapted from Kimberly S. Young, *Caught in the Net* (New York: John Wiley & Sons, 1998); James Nuernberg, "Internet As Addictive As Drugs," *Northeastern News*, 22 October 1997; and "Stuck in the Web," *Island Scene* Online, 1 January 1997; <www.islandscene.com>.

44. Information for this article adapted from Fred Stoeker and Stephen Arterburn, *Every Man's Battle: Winning the War on Sexual Temptation One Victory at a Time* (Colorado Springs: WaterBrook Press, 2000); and Tom Piotrowski, "Maximum Menace," *Youthculture,* winter 2000.

45. Information for this article adapted from Steve Watters, "Your Guide to Safer Surfing," *Plugged In,* June 2000; and Brendan Koerner, "A Lust for Profits," *U.S. News & World Report,* 27 March 2000.

46. Information for this article adapted from Guy Condon and David Hazard, *Fatherhood* Aborted (Wheaton, Ill.: Tyndale House Publishers, Inc., 2001).

47. Information for this article adapted from John W. Whitehead, "Does Abortion Lessen Crime—and Genius?" *Los Angeles Times,* 24 April 2001.

48. Information for this article adapted from Kristine Vick, "Throwaway Kids," CBNNews.com, 2 October 2000; and Genaro C. Armas, "Two Million Dads, 289,000 Moms Didn't Pay Child Support," Associated Press, 13 October 2000; <www.ap.org>.

49. Information for this article adapted from "Men Hurt Too," a brochure published by Hayes Publishing Co., Cincinnati, Ohio, 1997.

50. Information for this article adapted from "Unborn Children Respond to Pain at Ten Weeks," *The London Times,* August 2000; Patrick Goodenough, "Pro-Lifers Pounce on Calls to Anesthetize before Abortion," CNS News, 31 August 2000; and "Fetuses Have Short/Long-Term Memory, Doctors Say," Associated Press, 28 September 2000; <www.ap.org>.

51. Information for this article adapted from Candice McGarvey, "Jane Roe Was Won by Love," 12 June 2001; <www.crosswalk.com>.

52. Information for this article adapted from Lisa Girion, "Office Pressure Cookers Stewing Up 'Desk Rage,'" *Los Angeles Times,* 10 December 2000.

53. Information for this article adapted from Ashley Dunn, "Fairy Tale Falls Short for Rich," *Los Angeles Times,* 14 March 2000.

54. Information for this article adapted from Sonny Scarborough, "Ministering through God's Grace," *The Marketplace,* fall 2000.
55. Information for this article adapted from Randy Rowland, *The Sins We Love* (New York: Doubleday, 2000).
56. Information for this article adapted from "Credit Card Debt Can Affect Health," Reuters, 6 March 2000; <www.reuters.com>.
57. Information for this article adapted from Allison Samuels and David Noonan, "Baby's Booty," *Newsweek,* 4 December 2000.
58. Information for this article adapted from Jacques Steinberg, "Adults Side-step Serious Talks with Teenagers, Survey Finds," *New York Times,* 9 January 2001.
59. Information for this article adapted from Elizabeth Razzi, "Retailers' Siren Song," *Kiplinger's,* November 2000.
60. Information for this article adapted from Janet Bodnar, "Unspoiled Little Rich Kids," *Kiplinger's,* December 2000.
61. Information for this article adapted from <www.SFGate.com>, 9 March 2000.
62. Information for this article adapted from Sam Farmer, "A Losing Record for NCAA Whistle-Blower," *Los Angeles Times,* 30 March 2001.
63. Information for this article adapted from Alan Abrahamson, "Shame of the Games," *Los Angeles Times,* 7 January 2001.
64. Information for this article adapted from Susan Vaughn, "NFL Coach with Cerebral Palsy Has Winning Outlook," *Los Angeles Times Sunday* magazine, 5 November 2000.
65. Information for this article adapted from Alan Abrahamson, "Grand Kenyans," *Los Angeles Times,* 25 February 2001.
66. Information for this article adapted from Terry Beh, "An Unbroken Promise," an unpublished story from Promise Keepers Stand in the Gap conference.

67. Information for this article adapted from Jacqueline Trescott, "A Question of Color," *Parenting,* October 1996, 167.

68. Information for this article adapted from Jane Spencer, "Welcome to Happy Valley," *Newsweek,* 30 April 2001.

69. Information for this article adapted from Karen S. Peterson, "Black Couples Stay the Course," *USA Today,* 7 March 2000; and "Census Sketches Black Family," Associated Press, 14 February 2000; <www.ap.org>.

70. Information for this article adapted from Chuck Colson, "Book-Free Zone," 28 June 2001; <www.crosswalk.com>.

71. Information for this article adapted from Bill McCartney, *Sold Out* (Nashville: Word Publishing, 1997); and <http://alcoholism.about.com/health/alcoholism/library/blgetwell.htm>.

72. Information for this article adapted from Peg Tyre and Julie Scelfo, "A Car, a Call and a Terrible Crash," *Newsweek,* 14 May 2001; and "A Will to Live," *People,* 4 June 2001, 108–114.

73. Information for this article adapted from "Athletes' Rudeness Unchallenged," *Rocky Mountain News,* 6 February 2001.

74. Information for this article adapted from *The Best of Bits & Pieces* (Fairfield, N.J.: The Economics Press, Inc., 1994).

75. Information for this article adapted from "Working Ourselves to Death" and "This Is Your Brain without Sleep," <http://sleepdisorders.about.com>.

Contributing Writers

Marshall Allen – God has used several significant experiences to work in Marshall's life: his relationship with his wife, Sonja; three years spent as a missionary in Nairobi, Kenya; and his studies at Fuller Theological Seminary in Pasadena, California. He is a journalist for two newspapers in Glendale, California, *The Glendale News-Press* and *The Foothill Leader*, and a freelance writer. He and his wife are in the process of adopting a baby from Korea.

Tom Beard – Tom is a husband, father, and worship arts pastor in Castle Rock, Colorado. A former member of the Christian vocal group Glad, he is also an award-winning vocalist, keyboardist, songwriter, and arranger. Tom enjoys pickup sports, reading, jazz and R&B music, and chess. He is a rabid Oakland Raiders fan.

Terry Beh – Terry is the owner of Terry Beh Enterprises, a freelance business specializing in quality writing, editing, and photography. Prior to becoming a freelancer, Terry worked for seven years at Focus on the Family, becoming part of a team of top writers for Dr. James Dobson. After that, he served the ministry of Promise Keepers for five years as a member of its publications department and later as lead writer for founder and president Bill

McCartney. Terry lives in Castle Rock, Colorado, with his wife, Anne, and son, Christian.

Molly DeKruif — Molly has served as the senior editor for Promise Keepers radio broadcasts, including Bill McCartney's daily commentary, *4th and Goal,* since the program's inception in February 2000. In addition to writing, Molly loves decorating, reading, camping in the mountains, and long conversations with dear friends. Raised in Boulder, Colorado, she and her husband, Kristian, now reside in Denver.

Andy Fletcher — Andy is Young Life's International Schools deputy director, working to develop outreach relational programs to third culture kids worldwide. He has lived, traveled, spoken, and lectured abroad for much of his adult life. He writes for a number of Christian publications, including *Christianity Today*, *Youthworker Journal, Breakaway*, and others, has contributed to several books, and guest lectures on faith and science in public and international schools in the United States and overseas. He is married and has two teenagers.

Scott Gordon — Scott was a member of the original development team for the *4th and Goal* radio broadcast and served as Promise

Keepers radio executive producer. He has written radio and TV commercials, plays, and musical reviews, and was a published theater critic. Scott wishes to acknowledge the Lord Jesus Christ, from whom all good things come.

Jeff Leever – Jeff is manager of publications for Promise Keepers and author of the books *Daily Disciples* and the *Daily Disciples Study Guide* (with Dave Wardell). Jeff has served as Promise Keepers senior editor and is currently a content editor for *Men of Integrity*, a devotional magazine published by Christianity Today International. He holds a degree in English with an emphasis in writing from the University of Nebraska (Kearney). He has a wonderful wife, Erin, and an incredible daughter, Noelle. Contact Jeff at www.dailydisciples.com.

Don Morgan – Don graduated from Colorado State University with a degree in technical journalism/electronic reporting and a minor in European history. He currently serves as assistant to the president for writing with Focus on the Family and also writes for various organizations on a freelance basis. Don and his wife, Heather, reside in Colorado Springs, Colorado.

Craig Osten – Originally from northern California, Craig is the national director of team communications for the Alliance Defense Fund in Scottsdale, Arizona. Prior to his present position, he served as the assistant to Dr. James Dobson, president of Focus on the Family. He is married and has a ten-year-old daughter.

John T. Perrodin – John, an author, home-schooling father, and licensed attorney, currently serves as director of on-line editorial for Focus on the Family (www.family.org), where he has been a staff member for more than ten years. He thanks God for giving him the love, support, and inspiration of his amazing, artistic, home-schooling wife, Sue; the daily blessing of their children, Jace, Jenna Sue, Patch, Carol, and Quentin; and the constant encouragement of his parents, Tom and Helen Perrodin of Tucson, Arizona.

Additional contributor: **Charlie Richards.**

About *4th and Goal*

 *4th and Goal* is a daily three-minute radio commentary produced by the international men's ministry Promise Keepers. The program, subtitled *Coaching for Life's Tough Calls*, challenges men through a nonthreatening, hope-filled approach to everyday issues that men face. The commentaries address vital topics, such as parenting, the fatherless, teenage alienation, and marriage relationships, as well as report on breaking news and research related to men's daily interests. *4th and Goal* aims to reach the guy on the street—to give a message of hope and direction for life—and to raise the standard of integrity and masculinity that men live by.

Program Information

4th and Goal debuted on 145 stations across the United States on February 7, 2000, and by week's end was airing on 224 stations. *4th and Goal* is currently broadcast by more than 850 outlets.

Sign up to receive the daily *4th and Goal* message via e-mail on the Web at www.4thandgoal.org. Archived transcripts, station listings, resources, and other helpful information for men can also be found at www.4thandgoal.org.

If *4th and Goal* is not broadcast in your area, please call your local stations and request that they air the program as well as other Promise Keepers radio programs.

Radio stations interested in *4th and Goal* or other Promise Keepers radio programs, please call (303) 964-7799.

About Promise Keepers

 Promise Keepers is a Christian outreach aimed at building men of integrity. Through arena conferences, ongoing local small groups, educational seminars, resource materials, and local churches, Promise Keepers encourages men to live godly lives and to keep seven basic promises of commitment to God, their families, and fellow men. Promise Keepers seeks to unite Christian men of all races, denominations, ages, cultures, and socioeconomic groups, believing that accountable relationships among men are critical in helping one another become promise keepers in their relationships with God, their wives, their children, each other, and their communities.

History

On March 20, 1990, the head football coach for the University of Colorado, Bill McCartney, and his friend Dave Wardell, Ph.D., were on a three-hour car ride to a Fellowship of Christian Athletes meeting when they first discussed the idea of filling a stadium with Christian men. Later that year, seventy-two men began to fast and pray about the concept of thousands of men coming together for the purpose of Christian discipleship. In July 1991, forty-two hundred men gathered for the first Promise Keepers conference at the University of Colorado basketball arena. Since then, nearly five million men have attended more than one hundred Promise Keepers stadium and arena conferences.

Mission
Promise Keepers mission statement is direct and succinct: Men Transformed Worldwide.

Global Ministries
Promise Keepers has a growing international ministry, located on every continent, with activity in more than thirty countries. Events have been held in South Africa, Puerto Rico, Mexico, Costa Rica, Ghana, the Philippines, and other areas across the globe.

Promise Keepers continues to receive inquiries about developing men's ministries from countries around the world. More than one hundred thousand men have attended men's events directly related to Promise Keepers in countries outside the United States.

Local Small Groups
Across the country and around the world, hundreds of small groups of men continue to gather on a regular basis for Bible study and personal accountability. These local small groups are led independently

of Promise Keepers, but many use Promise Keepers resources for study and encouragement.

Resource Materials
Promise Keepers also develops and provides numerous resources for personal study and men's groups. These resources include audio/ video recordings, radio programs, books, study guides, worship tapes, and apparel.

Contact
For more information on Promise Keepers, please call (800) 888-7595, or visit our exciting Web site at www.promisekeepers.org.

About the Author

BILL MCCARTNEY is founder and president of the international men's ministry Promise Keepers and was the voice of the radio program *4th and* Goal from 2000–2002. He has a B.A. in education from the University of Missouri (1962) and is author of *4th and Goal PlayBook* (audio CD) with Jim Weidmann (Promise Keepers/Focus on the Family, 2001); *Sold Out Two-gether* with Lyndi McCartney (Word, 1998); *Sold Out* (Word, 1997); and *From Ashes to Glory* (Thomas Nelson, 1990, 1995). He was a contributing writer to the books *Seven Promises of a Promise Keeper* (Focus on the Family, 1994; Word, 1999); *Go the Distance* (Focus on the Family, 1996); and *What Makes a Man?* (NavPress, 1992).

McCartney is the former head football coach of the University of Colorado. His team won a conational championship in 1990. He has been inducted into the Colorado Sports Hall of Fame (1999) and the Orange Bowl Hall of Fame (1996) and has been honored as UPI Coach of the Year (1990), Big Eight Conference Coach of the Year (1985, 1989, 1990), and National Coach of the Year (1989).

He serves on the boards of directors of the Equip Foundation, Gospel to the Unreached Millions, and Concerts of Prayer International, and he has been honored with personal awards including: Humanitarian of the Year from the Syl Morgan Smith Colorado Gospel Music Academy (1999); the Evangelist Philip Award from the National Association of United Methodist Evangelists (1999); the Fire-Setters Award from Revival Fires Ministries (1997); Layperson of the Year from the National Association of Evangelicals (1996); ABC News Person of the Week (February 16, 1996); the Chief Award from Chief, Inc., Phoenix, Ariz. (1996); the Spectrum Award from *Sports Spectrum* magazine (1995); and the Impact America Award from Point Loma College (1995).

McCartney lives with his wife, Lyndi, in the Denver area. They have four children and eight grandchildren. The McCartneys attend Faith Bible Chapel, in Arvada, Colorado. He enjoys spending time with his family, golfing, and bike riding.

Also Available

4th and Goal PlayBook

Item # 27060111
Compact Disc with Study Guide
$5
Available today
1-800-888-7595
www.promisekeepers.org
www.4thandgoal.org

with Bill McCartney

Based on proven principles from Heritage Builders, this ten-part CD audio study series is designed for men's small-group use. What you'll find inside:

- Bill McCartney (Promise Keepers/*4th and Goal*) and Jim Weidmann (Focus on the Family/Heritage Builders) share personal struggles and insights;

- challenging discussion questions and practical ideas to help you become a better father;

- an easy-to-follow printed guide to discussion questions and Bible references;

- vital resources for fathers from Focus on the Family and Promise Keepers;

- a great small group resource!